accused

accused

R. Craig Smith:
The Spy Left
Out in the Cold

Norman R. Hamilton

Copyright © 1987 by
Horizon Publishers & Distributors, Inc.

All rights reserved. Reproduction in whole or any parts thereof in any form or by any media without written permission is prohibited.

ISBN: 0-88290-290-3
Library of Congress No.: 87-080150
Horizon Publishers Catalog & Order No.: 2010
First Printing, April 1987

Printed and distributed
in the United States of America by

& Distributors, Incorporated
50 South 500 West P.O. Box 490
Bountiful, Utah 84010-0490

Foreword

On April 4th, 1984, Richard Craig Smith was arrested by the FBI and accused of selling U.S. Army Intelligence secrets to agents of the Soviet KGB.

He was indicted by a grand jury in Alexandria, Virginia, then incarcerated in the Fairfax County jail for five weeks while his family and friends struggled to raise a half-million dollar bond to secure his freedom while awaiting trial.

The next twenty-three months were spent preparing for that trial, which began on April 7th, 1986 and ended four short days later.

He spent twenty-four months living under the threat of life imprisonment for spying against his own country, the United States of America.

Did Craig Smith actually sell out to the Soviets?

Did Craig Smith tell the truth about being recruited by the CIA for an amazing spy operation in Japan?

Did Craig Smith really love his country as he claimed, or did he sell his military knowledge to the enemy for a few pieces of silver?

* * * * *

The story begins at eleven o'clock on the morning of Friday, April 11, 1986, eight-and-a-half hours after Federal Judge Richard L. Williams gave his final instructions to the jury, when nine women and three men filed out of the jury box and retired to the jury room to begin their deliberations.

Craig Smith. Photo by Craig Fuji courtesy of Seattle Times.

Table of Contents

Foreword 7
Photo Credits 12
1 The Verdict 13
2 My Background, Early Years, and Marriage 16
3 A Career in Intelligence 25
4 Recruited by the CIA 33
5 A New Business Career 43
6 The First CIA Mission to Tokyo 47
7 My Wife Susan 62
8 The Second CIA Mission to Tokyo 68
9 Left Out in the Cold 79
10 The FBI Investigation 88
11 My Arrest and Imprisonment 105
12 My Attorneys are Selected 121
13 Freed on $500,000 Bond 131
14 The Search for the Truth 139
15 The Fight to Have the Truth Admitted 149
16 Preparing for the Trial 155
17 The Trial Begins 160
18 Our Defense Bogs Down 170
19 Our Defense is Resurrected 177
20 Closing Arguments 187
21 My Faith is Tested 191
22 The Verdict 194
23 The Aftermath 200
24 My Feelings 208
25 Did God Work a Miracle? 211
26 How Can We Prevent This From Happening Again? 216

Photo Credits

1. Craig Smith. Craig Fuji/Seattle Times 9
2. The La Scala Coffee Shop 51
3. The Takanawa Tobu Hotel 52
4. The Soviet Embassy commercial compound gate 54
5. The Westin Ilikai Hotel in Waikiki. Westin Ilikai 64
6. Susan and Craig Smith. 67
7. The Westin St. Francis Hotel in San Francisco.
   Westin St.Francis. 69
8. The Miko Coffee Shop 71
9. The Federal Building in Seattle.
   Larry Dion/Seattle Times 94
10. The FBI Headquarters Building in Washington D.C.
    Lisa C. Ure 99
11. The FBI field office in Alexandria. Lisa C. Ure 106
12. The Fairfax County Courthouse in Alexandria.
    Lisa C. Ure 107
13. The walkway to the Fairfax County Courthouse.
    Lisa C. Ure 109
14. The attorneys 126
15. The defense team 157
16. Dr. Sherry Skidmore and Craig Smith 202
17. Smith Family 203
18. The Smith family home in Bellevue 205

1

The Verdict

Susan and I were now alone in the witness room, just down the hall from the courtroom where eight-and-a-half hours before, federal prosecutors had ruthlessly hammered the jury in a brutal closing argument.

Piercing words of accusation had been spoken: "Betrayal!" "Treason!" Condescending words of self-righteousness: "Now ask yourself, would this great nation—the United States of America—leave one of its own citizens out in the cold if he were truly in the service of his country?" My head still throbbed from their verbal savagery.

All I could think of was the real and imminent possibility that I could spend every remaining minute of my mortal life in a federal prison.

I thought of my briefcase lying on the table before me, full of my case evidence. If convicted, could I take it with me? No, of course not. I found myself nervously emptying it out, preparing for the worst possibility.

More thoughts raced through my head. If the worst came, what about my family? How could I guide and influence my children's growth from behind a locked cell door? From a federal prison?

"Susan," I struggled, "we've got to plan for the kids. Now! Sunny's almost 13. Brittanie and Ian are still pretty flexible, but I don't know about Aubrey. Five is pretty young to figure out why Daddy's not coming home again...." My voice was breaking, and I choked back tears as I tried to get my mind on positive ground again. The fatigue of the eleven relentless hours since the time court convened at nine o'clock that morning had left us both weak and exhausted.

The hall and adjoining rooms slowly emptied as evening approached. They were now silent. Gone from the witness room were our families—our parents, our brothers and sisters. Gone now, leaving us alone with our thoughts and our private words together.

Gone also from the hallway were most of those who had argued against me, the FBI and federal prosecutors. Earlier, we were forced to listen to their noisy, profane voices planning their "victory celebration." Only two were left now, and their occasional jokes and comments echoed in the corridor. Almost everyone was gone now, except Susan and me.

My heart ached as I looked into Susan's tear-swollen eyes. Did my wife still believe in my innocence of crimes of which my government had accused me, that of selling U.S. government secrets to a Soviet agent for a few thousand dollars? If I were convicted, could Susan continue to believe the truth about how I risked my life for my country—truth that I could never document to her because of government classification?

Suddenly we heard footsteps in the quiet hallway outside the door. We heard the by now familiar voice of the bailiff talking to a reporter. "We have a verdict," said the voice. Our hearts sank.

Our attorneys had warned us that when a verdict comes in early, it's usually guilty. They had hoped the jury would struggle with the case for two to four days and finally reach a not guilty verdict.

We returned anxiously to the courtroom and soon heard the entire jury moving down the hall. We remembered our instructions: look them in the eye as they filed into the courtroom. If the verdict were to go against me, they wouldn't look back at me—and they didn't.

THE VERDICT

Each of the nine women and three men passed by me, avoiding my eyes.

After they had taken their seats, Judge Williams asked, "Have you reached a verdict on all five counts of the indictment?"

"We have, your honor."

My throat tightened.

"Will the bailiff please hand the verdict to the clerk of the court."

My stomach knotted as the clerk then passed the paper to the judge. He read it thoroughly without the slightest hint as to its content. I looked intently at his face but could discern nothing. I felt a flush come over my face as he intoned a warning against loud or emotional outbursts from the audience as the verdict was read.

I felt my last hope was gone. He was preparing the courtroom for a verdict of guilty.

The judge handed the paper to the court clerk.

"The defendant will please rise and face the jury."

The pressure was so intense I could barely move. One of my two attorneys, Brent Carruth, helped me to my feet. My heart was pounding and my ears were ringing. My mind flashed to the worst. I would never again hold my wife in my arms: never again, for the rest of my life on this earth, would I feel the sweetness of the love of our four children around the circle of our family.

"Will the clerk of the court please read the verdict."

The clerk stood, cleared her throat, and began reading. "On the first count, we find the defendant, Richard Craig Smith. . . ."

2

My Background, Early Years & Marriage

I was born in Logan, Utah, on November 20th, 1943, the second of seven children of Hyrum Mack Smith II and Dorothy Monson Smith. I was a child of the war.

My very earliest memories are those of standing on the grass outside our little house in Jacksonville, Florida, after World War II and watching "my Dad's" Navy planes fly directly toward me and then straight overhead. I was only three, but I knew he was flying one of them as a U. S. Navy flight instructor. I even fantasized that he reached out the window and waved to me with his hat.

I was fascinated with uniforms. Two favorite photographs of my father were one of him in his navy officer's dress blue uniform, and another of him in the Scottish kilts that he'd brought back from his church mission to Scotland. Was my thirteen-year career with Army Intelligence thus somehow foreordained?

After the war, the family returned to Salt Lake City; I grew up in my grandfather's old home on Fifth East. My favorite memory of that house was climbing the old cherry tree in the front yard. This was a fine old house my grandfather built, but was destroyed in 1952, when I was nine. A contractor who undertook to dig a basement underneath the house had miscalculated, and had collapsed a foundation wall. While it stood, it was a museum of memories and family traditions. I still can feel the softness of the heavy red draperies and see the long staircase with busts of Joseph Smith and Brigham Young at the bottom.

Dad had to finish college while working at two—and sometimes three—jobs. He was an example of industry and sacrificed for the future and for his family. He'd go down to the creamery and load milk trucks from three to seven a.m., then go on to school or work at the hospital from seven to three p.m., and finally spend three till ten p.m. selling sporting-goods at the big Sears store. He'd study from ten until midnight and then start over again at three a.m.

My parents really loved and cared for us. Perhaps that's my most cherished memory of growing up in Salt Lake City. My mother got her talent for loving and caring for a big family of seven of us children from her mother because that's the way she was raised.

There were wonderful memories of vacations, all nine of us and the dog too, packed into the station wagon on our way to southern California or to Yellowstone. But the most special moments and memories were in my grandfather's big house, while it stood—memories of my mother making the long trek up the stairs to see that prayers were said and to sing us softly to sleep.

There was a song a few years back that described what life was like for us in Salt Lake City. A line in the song talks about a home where a man could have a boy, and a boy could have a dog, and the yard went on forever. That was how I remembered growing up. It seemed that days were always sunny.

When I was about eleven, there was one incident that had an impact on my later life. Grandma Augusta Monson, Mom's mother, was able to get tickets to hear Herbert Philbrick speak at the Salt Lake Tabernacle on Temple Square. He'd been recruited by the Soviets, who had attempted to get him to betray his country. The FBI set him up as a double agent.

It was in 1954, during the postwar Communist build-up in Europe, that he related his experiences of danger and intrigue, how he couldn't tell his family what he was doing, and how his wife accidentally discovered his cache of reports and, out of fear, started to burn them. His story later became a number one radio and television series entitled, "I Led Three Lives."

I sat there enthralled and experienced the same feelings of pride in my country—of a desire to take risks for my country—that propelled me into a similar double-agent role with the KGB nearly thirty years later.

In 1958 Dad and Mom took Hy and me to Washington D.C., where Dad spoke at a White House Conference on Children and Youth. This was my first trip east. I stood for the first time in the Lincoln Memorial, tears staining my cheeks. There was the solitude and endlessness of Arlington Cemetery. All of our lives we'd been taught patriotism and loyalty to our wonderful country, and suddenly we were in the midst of its major symbols. It was as if Dad stood between us, put his hands on our shoulders and said, "Boys, this is what I mean!"

As a result of his outstanding White House talk my father was offered a job with what is now the Department of Education. All the way home however, he would say to Mother, "I can't do it," only to hear her positive reply, "Yes, you can." They would lead the family in prayer for a decision, always asking for "what's best for the family."

* * * * *

It was in 1959 that we moved to the Washington D.C. area and made our new home in Virginia, very near the scene of my later arrest, and I finished my last two years of high school there. We became part of the Washington scene and made many new friends, most of whom held the same patriotic views my parents had instilled us.

MY BACKGROUND, EARLY YEARS & MARRIAGE

The bishop of our ward (church congregation) knew that I needed to find work to save money for a church mission and arranged for me to apply for a job at graduation with his government agency, the CIA, where I was eventually employed as a microphotographer.

After nine months with the Agency I served a two year mission in Paris, France. Returning home, I entered Brigham Young University. I intended to major in psychological counseling and English, but since the draft called me during the Vietnam War, I enlisted in the Army in 1967. Partly due to my language skills and security clearance with the CIA, I was eventually assigned to the Army Security Agency where we monitored radio signals throughout the world.

It was fascinating work, but it became a bit routine after many months, so I requested a transfer to the Intelligence Branch of the Army as a counterintelligence special agent. They transferred me to Arizona for agent training, and then they sent me to Monterey, California, for language school, where I took one year of intensive Japanese.

On the way to Arizona a funny thing happened. I stopped in Provo, Utah, to see my brothers and my sister Terry. She talked me into a blind date—for a hamburger at the A & W with one of her close friends. It was against my better judgment, so I went grubby and unshaven.

When Susan Woods walked into the room, I realized that I had made a mistake. What a lovely girl! We lingered over that hamburger until two in the morning, and five months of letters and phone calls later, in July of 1972, we were married in the Mormon Temple in Logan, Utah. Our two-day trip to Monterey was our honeymoon because I had to be in language school the following Monday in the morning. We were so happy and so in love.

We moved into a small apartment in Pacific Grove, on the famous Monterey Peninsula of California. We enjoyed walking to the beach overlooking Monterey Bay and watching the sea otters frolic in the surf. Someone asked me if we ever saw the famous monarch butterflies that return to Pacific Grove every year. Well, we lived on Monarch Point, near the Monarch Inn. We saw monarch butterflies by the thousands that year.

Language school was tough, day after day, eight o'clock to four-thirty in class, plus three hours of study every night. We cherished our weekends together.

We were very active in our ward, and met a delightful new friend there by the name of Joseph Smith. He was from Canada and a psychiatrist by profession. I later sought his help, just before my arrest for spying, hopefully to convince the FBI to evaluate my story under truth serum. More later about Dr. Smith's role in that endeavor.

By the end of the school year in June of 1973, Susan went to Denver to her parents' home to have our first baby. I had to report to my assignment in Tokyo, and Susan couldn't travel until after the baby was born. Fortunately, I found a house near the Army base where I was to work and then flew back to Denver in time for our daughter, Sunny, to greet the world.

When Susan and our new baby were ready to fly to Japan to join me there, I was a bit concerned about a young mother coping with international travel. After all, she was raised in Phoenix and Denver and had never traveled except to college at Rexburg, Idaho and Provo, Utah.

I needn't have worried. Susan, I learned, was a very adaptable person. To take a newborn child and set out to make a new home for us in a foreign country was a challenge she took in stride. I respected that courage.

Japan was good to the three Smiths. Brittanie, our second daughter, was born in 1976, the year we moved back to the U.S. Again, Susan flew to Denver for the occasion, and I was able to be there, too. After three-and-a-half years in Tokyo, we were transferred back to Army Intelligence Headquarters near Washington D. C. in 1976.

* * * * *

MY BACKGROUND, EARLY YEARS & MARRIAGE

In the spring of 1984, while sitting in a Fairfax, Virginia jail, I had a long time to think about events that strengthened my role as the head of our family, events that led up to my leaving Army Intelligence, and events that brought my wife and children through our crisis of trial by fire. Each time, my thoughts returned to Susan's strength, steadfastness, and loyalty to her family.

It's not always like this. By far, most Army intelligence officers are either single or they're divorced after a few years of marriage. This is because of the incredible stress placed on the average intelligence officer's home life by the constant pressures of secrecy. These marriages crack from the strain of his frequent disappearances for hours or days and by the forced lack of communication.

Our marriage survived because we were able to maintain life's basics: Who are we? Where did we come from? Where are we going? How are we going to get there? And most important of all, with whom are we going to make this journey?

Even when Susan and I were first dating by phone and letter, she knew I was in training in Arizona to become a special agent in intelligence. In fact, much of what I was learning was open to her. She knew I was being given intensive education about other countries' cultures, political systems, and intelligence techniques. Certainly there were no secrets about intensive study of the Japanese language during our first year of marriage.

As a matter of fact, my first six months in Tokyo were fairly open. I was permitted to share with her what I was doing in my first assignments, maintaining the security of our section of the base, briefing and teaching others about security details, and conducting tests to try to penetrate our security.

It was during my second six months in Japan that the curtain began to wrap tightly around my activities, and Susan could only be "married to half of me." Wives of intelligence officers are forbidden to probe into their husbands' activities. Our section held a special limited security briefing for all agents' wives. Susan was told wives could only support their husbands by ignoring their erratic hours and secretive behavior. It was at this point in my career that Susan was beginning to understand the immensity and importance of what I had chosen to do. She was awed and a little puzzled by it all.

It was at the beginning of our second six months in Tokyo that I was plunged into the inner sanctum of intelligence operations in Japan, working directly with the case officers. They, in turn, handled the people in the field, many of whom were double agents. Our mission was to support the U.S. military services in Japan and Korea. Often I would disappear for an afternoon or a day or two days—totally disappear. I had no freedom to come home and share my experiences with my wife. Understandably, it was difficult for both of us.

I was becoming involved, too, in what we call "tradecraft," which refers to all of the techniques, the tools, the equipment, the codes—everything that physically goes into any clandestine operation. I was invited to come in and provide tradecraft support to the case officers, and I learned quickly and enjoyed my work.

Ultimately, my superiors assigned me to support a small, elite group of double agents, and I began to prepare to become a case officer myself. It was at this point that Susan was really put to the test and came through magnificently. Susan had to have the same confidence in me every day for the next six years. More significantly, this faith and trust carried our marriage through its greatest test: my indictment by a federal grand jury for spying.

It is difficult to imagine the anxiety and pressure placed upon the children in such a family as mine.

"Where's Daddy?"

"Why doesn't he call?"

"Did he forget it's my birthday?"

"He doesn't care or he would have remembered!"

The difficulty was that in my having to compensate for round one of secrecy, I'd set up even more stress for everyone involved. Then in round two I'd have to excuse, explain, apologize, and even lie about round one. I'm thankful for a faithful, trusting wife and four very resilient children. They probably saved both the family and our marriage by learning to accept as routine the insecurity of the unknown and the uncertain.

It might be asked, "Why doesn't the intelligence community fill its ranks with good, resilient people who can handle marriage, family and career with maturity?" They'd probably like to.

In reality, all of the intelligence services—the military, CIA, FBI, and others recruit heavily at Christian schools. Graduates from these schools are the very kind of bright, mature people who have conservative values, patriotic feelings, strong marriages, no police records, freedom from drug or alcohol problems, and often a foreign language.

They fit the desired profile perfectly, especially those who have returned from domestic or foreign missions, Peace Corps assignments and the like. Many do respond and join these agencies for the same reasons I did. They offered a chance to further our education and growth, an opportunity to serve our country, and a great way to see more of this earth we live on.

However, there is a downside. Few agents from conservative backgrounds can survive this type of career for more than a few years. In the first place, they cannot forever be torn away from their companions and their children like a balloon jerked back on a string. Eventually it becomes more and more difficult to come to grips with the constant duplicity they must always be involved in to protect their own lives as well as those of their colleagues. The attrition rate of conservative, church-going, intelligence agents is high, as is the divorce rate among all intelligence officers.

Our marriage, too, was subjected to the stresses and pressures of my clandestine work. With the arrival of three children during my years as an agent, I sometimes wonder that we had so few problems. But we managed to keep our perspective that marriage was everlasting, realizing that there was much more to our relationship than living together and raising children.

Susan and I both believe deeply that our children's future depends on our nation's security, and that the opportunity to fulfill their life long goals would be threatened by the loss of our country's freedom. So our feelings would come around full circle. The sacrifices we made within our family circle were justified by the needs of our national survival—needs for our children's future.

Thus we walked this thin line for the first nine years of our marriage, and with our shared understanding, we managed to make it in spite of the odds against us.

3

A Career in Intelligence

When I arrived in Washington, D.C., in 1978 for my new assignment, I learned that our headquarters office had a world wide operational responsibility, as opposed to a highly localized operation in Japan. Our work at Headquarters permitted us to pass on the less important cases to the field offices and handle the more significant cases from Washington, so I saw a dramatic expansion of our operational range and an upgrading of our priority levels. We worked major operations throughout most of the world.

When our family first arrived in the Washington, D.C. area, we rented a small apartment in Laurel, Maryland, near my new office. After six months we were so sure we would remain at headquarters for at least five or six years that we bought our first home. It was a two-story brick Cape Cod cottage in Severn, Maryland. We didn't realize that a major promotion and transfer were in store for us just one year later. I had just converted from active duty to civilian status within the Department of Defense. As such, presumably I could stay at headquarters for as long as I performed well.

Meanwhile, we loved our new home. We adopted an Irish setter puppy, a gift from Susan's parents. He played with our two girls in the large back yard, which reminded me of the endless back yard of my youth at our family home in Salt Lake City. I recalled thinking of the day I returned to that home of my childhood years later, and found that the "endless" back yard had shrunk drastically. I wondered how the big back yard behind our Cape Cod home in Maryland would look to our children some day.

It was now 1978. We'd been in our new home a year and expected to stay there for many more, but suddenly the head agent in the San Francisco field office announced his retirement. He'd been there several years, but the field office had never been developed to its full potential. We wondered who would be selected to replace him, to move up to just about the choicest field assignment in Special Operations.

Still being one of the new kids on the block at headquarters, I gave no thought to the San Francisco job. There were several others who had more seniority or were more qualified. I was understandably surprised when the Chief of Operations called me into his office and asked, "Do you want to go to San Francisco?"

I asked "Why me?"

He told me that they wanted someone more aggressive, someone who could maintain his intensity in the work, someone who could build that office and its caseload to its maximum potential.

"If you want it, I'll go to bat with the old man."

I said I'd talk it over with my wife. After all, it was a big jump and in many ways was probably over my head.

Susan simply said, "Let's go!"

Noel Jones, the chief, sold the top man on my going to the new job, and in thirty days' time we'd packed and moved to San Ramon, California, near Oakland, and I began commuting to the Federal Building in San Francisco.

It's important to have a basic understanding of ranks and promotions for both the military and civilians in Army Intelligence. First of all, the traditional rankings of commissioned and non-commissioned officers don't carry as much weight as in other branches of the military. I was only an enlisted Spec-4 when I was invited into Special Operations, alongside commissioned and warrant officers, while serving in Japan. Often warrant officers directed lieutenants and captains. When I left the Army and transferred to civilian status, still more doors were opened because civilians could be promoted even more independently of military rank.

The San Francisco assignment was a great opportunity and challenge. Shortly after my arrival there, Headquarters closed the only other field office they had west of the Mississippi, with the result that my office in San Francisco covered all midwest and western states, including Alaska and Hawaii. When we took over the cases from the Southwestern Office, we had far more double-agent cases per officer and a wider scope and range of activities than any other office, including headquarters and most FBI field offices. I was a case officer, responsible for as many as fifteen operations at once.

My boss had mentioned the phrase "intense view of the work" when he chose me for San Francisco. He was right. I became intensely absorbed in developing a high level of activity. In fact, because of the increasing caseload, they soon sent me an assistant, and we each had a number of cases going.

I was relatively free to take the office in any direction I wanted, and I loved this freedom. For the first twelve months I felt I was doing what my talents were meant for me to do even though I demanded much of myself.

There were three reasons for such an effort on my part. With the newness of the job, I wanted to excel, I wanted to prove myself. I wanted to meet and exceed the expectations of those at Headquarters who chose me for this job. When they closed the office in the southwest U.S., they did so because of a declining caseload. The remaining cases were important enough to be transferred to my office, and I felt responsible to give them my best management. Last of all I could, and ultimately did, increase the caseload on my own, raising the productivity of the office and bringing it closer to its full potential, which was Headquarter's objective in the first place.

I'm only permitted to give you very general information about what we did as case officers in the San Francisco field office. When a person, perhaps an enlisted or commissioned member of the Army, or a citizen of this country or another country, approached the Army and told our side that they'd been approached by the other side for information, the case would be assigned by Headquarters to the appropriate field office.

We'd pursue this contact with the objective of establishing him as a double agent to help us find exactly how the other side was attempting to penetrate the Army's security. Similar offices were maintained by the Departments of Air Force and Navy (including Marines), as well as the FBI and CIA. Cases came to us from these and other government agencies as well, and we in turn referred cases to them as might be appropriate.

I took advantage of every opportunity to initiate double-agent operations. Perhaps we would dangle someone in front of the people on the other side, hoping they'd take the bait.

In any event, my assistant and I would each have a dozen or so operations going at once. We didn't maintain daily or even weekly contact; sometimes we'd see our agent only once a month or so. This was due to the need for secrecy in communicating with them. Their lives were at stake, so we devised all manner of rendezvous in bars, hotel lobbies, or terminals, wherever we could. We used signals designed to insure safety. If either of us lit a cigarette, it meant danger —perhaps we were being watched—and the meeting was aborted.

I did light cigarettes, and even ordered drinks, but I didn't smoke the cigarettes or drink the drinks as these activities were foreign to my Mormon upbringing. Leading a life of constant deceit and duplicity called for careful and thorough security measures, and we had to do whatever it took to make it work. After all, our lives and operations were on the line, so we tackled these extraordinary projects with extraordinary methods.

Someone once defined counterespionage as "an acid trip in a hall of mirrors." Eric Ambler called it the "game of games" in his book "Light of Day." Everyone in counterespionage must play dirty. We only asked ourselves two questions: "Will it work?" and "Can we deny it?" Our aim was to pull it off without losing a life or blowing someone's cover. If detected, we or our proxies would stonewall and deny that it ever happened.

I had a plaque on my desk for some years. It read:

> "I think that if I were asked to single out one specific group of men, one type, one category, as being the most suspicious, unbelieving, unreasonable, petty, inhuman, sadistic, double-crossing set of bastards in any language, I would say without hesitation, 'The people who run counterespionage departments.' "
>
> —Eric Ambler
> *Light of Day*

I mentioned that agents with a strong Christian orientation find it difficult to live a lie for very many years. Actually it's fascinating to look back at just how agents and their case officers slip into the duplicity mold without even realizing what's happening to them. First an honest, God-fearing person will resist the dishonest aspects of intelligence work. Then he(she) tolerates it as a means to an end, because the end is a worthy and patriotic cause. Finally, the agent actually embraces deception, extra-legal activity, and duplicity in exchange for the tangible results which are obtainable thereby.

During the first few months, the caseload in San Francisco increased above my expectations. I was receiving a great deal of personal satisfaction from my efforts and was feeling that I'd paid the price to work among the best. I gained a sense of accomplishment and the pride of achievement. Pats on the back came from the people who trusted me and gave me my big chance in my career. For the first twelve months in San Francisco, only the sky was my limit. I felt as if I were at the top of my chosen profession.

Susan knew how much I loved my work and how much personal satisfaction I was getting from it, but I was away from home a lot, constantly on the road to everywhere. I was unable to share any of my success details with my wife.

I used to think that someday I would write a novel about the life of an intelligence officer's wife. I would title it "Her Husband's Mistress." As time passed, jealousy did begin to be a factor although it was minor at first. At this twelve-months-in-San-Francisco milepost, Susan was six months pregnant with our first son, and events began to move me away from the brass ring of success in the career I loved so much.

I began to realize how much I was neglecting my wife and family. I should have realized it all along even if I couldn't have done anything to change things yet. Now I seriously began to ask myself how I could find a balance between wife and family and my "jealous mistress"—my career in Army Intelligence.

During Susan's final three months of pregnancy with Ian, I was more and more torn between my work and my family. Until my arrest and indictment in 1984, five years later, this was the most agonizing time of my life.

One day I looked at the words on the plaque on my desk, the one that described counterintelligence officers, and almost got sick! Was that how I would be remembered? A new thought process was beginning.

A major hurdle for intelligence people is that they have no close friends. I frequently felt concerned about this. Mike Davis was an exception. Mike was about my age and a police officer, a night cop, one of the best. SWAT-team, trained hostage negotiator, rape-crisis task-force—he handled all the tough jobs. He was also an active member of my church. Mike's family was very much like ours in size and ages of children.

Because our work was so similar, we could talk to each other, not about operations, but about the effect our work had on our lives and our families. Occasionally I'd ride in his cruiser at night just to talk. We were both troubled by the same problem of our careers vs. our families. The more we talked, the more we yearned to be normal husbands and fathers again. We told ourselves over and over again that we should go back to our families. Then I'd read that piercing message on the plaque again, and I'd say, that's not where I want to be.

I wanted to go home to Salt Lake City and be normal again. I wanted to be like everyone else. I was tired of pretending to be so many people. I was torn. I wanted to be a loving father and husband in Salt Lake City and surround myself and my family with a loving home and all the trappings of normalcy. Then Ian was born.

* * * * *

My first son was special. I realize that most fathers feel the same way about their sons. This little baby meant more than I could put into words. I wanted him to grow up close to me and be my friend and companion. I wanted my son to have the same feeling about his father that I had about my Dad.

Ian was born slightly jaundiced, so we had to leave him in the hospital for a week. Seeing him there in the nursery, I felt a special sweetness. Ian was different.

When Susan took him in for his two week checkup, she called me at the office, and told me in an anxious voice, "Ian's got blood problems, and we're taking him to the hospital. Can you come?"

"Yes, in a little while," I replied.

Before I could get away, she called again. "We're at the hospital, and Ian's bilirubin count is high—way too high. Come quickly!"

Doctors don't know exactly what causes this condition, but it's an indication of a liver malfunction, and it's especially dangerous in newborn babies.

When I arrived at the hospital, I realized we faced a crisis for Ian. A normal count is twelve. Eighteen is dangerous, and Ian's was twenty-five to twenty-six. Brain damage was a possibility, and this was serious.

The doctor said, "He's got to be at Oakland Children's Hospital within an hour for a complete blood exchange. Normally we'd call for an ambulance. Would you rather drive him?"

"Yes," I answered, and stepped to a telephone and called Mike to help me give my baby boy a healing blessing through the priesthood power that we both hold. Mike's wife Sherry called him in from the tennis court, and we blessed Ian right there in their living room, on the way to Children's Hospital.

When we arrived, the medical technicians quickly typed Ian's blood to be sure of matching it correctly, and the count was down to eighteen. This baffled them, so they drew a full sample, and it read sixteen.

They called back to the first hospital with their count, and asked for a recount of the original blood sample. It was still twenty-six! I remember that our doctor was actually embarrassed. We told him that we had blessed our child, and he seemed to understand although he explained that under optimum recovery, the count would only go down one or two per hour. Ian's count dropped from twenty-six to sixteen to twelve within about one hour's time.

This experience was a turning point in my life. That night I slept peacefully for the first time in many months. There was no question left in my heart or mind. Nothing was more important than my family. The decision was made. I had experienced spiritual assurances when I pronounced the blessing on Ian. These assurances had nothing to do with Ian's health—they had only to do with me. The Lord had just rapped me on the knuckles and said, "Why are you having a problem with this?"

I called Headquarters a few days later to announce my resignation. I agreed to stay until the end of 1979 and left Army Intelligence in January of 1980, thirteen years after I'd first enlisted.

Mike Davis left his police career about this same time. The two of us took a group of Explorer Scouts up into Utah's High Uinta Mountains in September, a month after Ian's recovery, and we hatched our career plans while sitting in a tent in a high mountain meadow.

4

Recruited by the CIA

Twenty-two months later, on July 28th, 1981, at 8:15 P.M., I was sitting in my room in the New Otani Hotel in Tokyo when the telephone rang. A gentleman's voice on the other end of the line said, "This is Ken White from the U. S. Embassy."

Actually, this turned out to be the exact date and time when I was recruited by the Central Intelligence Agency of the U. S. government to serve my country as a double agent in what was intended to be one of the deepest penetrations ever made into the Soviet KGB.

How I got to Tokyo is a long story, but let's get back to Ken White. He said, "Mr. Smith, I'd like to meet you. Would you have time right now?"

I was there on civilian business, and I assumed he was with the commercial section of the embassy. Perhaps he had missed out on a previous briefing I'd given for them. I was anxious to oblige and agreed to meet with him. A short time later he knocked on the door of my room.

Ken White was an average-looking American with a companion who appeared to be Japanese. He was introduced as Danny Ishida, but I was never sure whether the first letter of his name was a "U," an "A," or an "I." Ishida spoke very little, but when he did, it was obvious that he was an American, too, because his speech gave no trace of his having come from outside the United States.

They asked me about how my company was doing and about the upcoming trade mission to Tokyo that we had announced for twelve Utah firms, to be held in October of that year. They knew quite a bit about why I was in Japan this trip, and Ken White referred by name to a Japanese officer in the commercial section of the embassy.

"Mr. Ushijima said he's really impressed with your list of Utah companies coming on the mission. I guess you've done a dynamite job of preparation."

Then White began mentioning names of other people, not only in the embassy but in the intelligence community I'd known in the past. This was my first indication that these were no ordinary "vanilla-flavored" commercial section attaches.

Then Ken White changed the subject slightly. "Mr. Smith, you were in the service here in Japan some time ago, weren't you?"

I replied, "Yes, but I wasn't directly associated with the service even though I was on active duty because I worked for Army Intelligence."

"Then you must have worked with Ted Marshall?" (This was not his true name.)

At first it didn't hit me, but then I realized they were talking about a counterintelligence agent I knew, calling him by his true name and not his cover name. In fact, I was surprised they would bring up his name so casually.

I said, "How do you know Ted Marshall?"

"Oh, we've known Ted for quite a while. We've done some things with Ted."

That was when the first flag went up. I said, "I get the feeling that this conversation is going in some direction other than about a trade mission."

White said, "Well, I'm sorry we couldn't come right up front with you, but you know how the game is played."

He went on, "We're aware of your work for the Army when you were here before, and Marshall tells us you were very good at what you did."

That was a nice compliment, coming from some one I respected as much as Ted Marshall, but I was more interested in how they knew so much about me. I said, "Wait a minute. Who are you guys?"

Ken White said, "Craig, we're from the Agency."

More correctly, he referred to the Agency by the organizational cover name it uses for its Japan operations. That name is classified, and I cannot use it here. I can mention that it's an acronym, or block of letters (or was, because they change these code names every few years).

When they said they were from the CIA, I said, "How do I know that?"

Ken White pulled a folded piece of paper from his inside coat pocket. He said, "Before we get into that I'll have to get you to sign a standard security agreement." Again he added, "You know how the game is played."

Now my curiosity was really aroused, so having nothing to lose, I signed the familiar form. Still wary, however, I said, "I'm still not convinced you are who you say you are. Anyone could show a security form."

"Well," Ken said, "Now that you've signed the agreement, I think we'll be able to satisfy you that we are who we say we are."

He proceeded to unfold extensive information about what I did in my intelligence career. In fact, they were so familiar with my personnel file and other sensitive matters, they had to be from the Agency.

I still had to make sure, so for twenty minutes or more we compared detailed notes on cases I'd handled, agents I'd managed, and so on. I was finally convinced enough to ask them a tentative question. "Well, what do you want of me?"

"Not very much. Craig, we'd just like you to serve as a courier for us, to deliver certain packages and messages back to the U.S.

We'd like you to assist us in an operation we're working on; this is to be carried on in the course of your normal activity while traveling to Japan."

Ken White consistently used my middle name as I'd always been known to my friends. This was an important indicator that they were on the inside because all my records showed the name, "Richard C. Smith." Furthermore, I couldn't get over the fact that the names and dates and places they were mentioning couldn't have been known to outsiders.

What really made me curious was why they had chosen me—especially in light of an incident which took place during my exit interview with the Chief of Operations, Noel Jones, in San Francisco just a couple years before. This happened when I left Army Intelligence to enter the business world.

He was visibly upset. He didn't accept any of my family reasons for leaving the service. I recall that he himself was in a second marriage that was going downhill, and he simply expected everyone in Army Intelligence to sacrifice his personal life for the cause. The fact that I had left after only eighteen months in San Francisco had convinced him that I had walked out on him.

I remember his words. He said that he would "personally see to it" that I would never work for the U.S. government again. I had thought of his words many times since that conversation because they meant that if I failed in private business, I could never go back to the government for a job.

Either he changed his mind when the CIA did a background investigation on me or they never made contact with him because here was my government at my door, asking me to work for them again—this time for the CIA.

I had to be absolutely sure that they were who they said they were—agents of the CIA—before I would become involved with them. I asked a lot of questions about names and places out of my past experiences. In the intelligence community we call this process the interrogative challenge. I needed to validate their credentials. I wanted to know what they knew; their answers could prove them to be authentic. Many innocent people have been suckered into "false flag" operations by failing to follow this precaution. It was not inconceivable that these people were even working for the KGB.

They came through with the right answers every time, and I was satisfied beyond doubt that they were who they said they were. I didn't ask to see badges or documents of any kind because if they were phonies, they'd have them anyway. Remember the term "tradecraft"? Credentials are easy to come by, so they're relatively meaningless in this kind of work.

In my first conversation with them, I recognized the specific steps of recruiting an agent for the U.S. cause. I had done this many times myself. First was the process of identifying the right person for the job and then assessing his value as an agent, considering the niche in the world where he lives, works, travels and the people he deals with. Before ever contacting him, he would be carefully "vetted," a word we use privately in our work to refer to deep assessment or qualifying to determine if the source would be loyal. We had to know he would perform, especially under pressure.

If everything checked out, the individual would be approached, though not necessarily as directly as I was. The approach might be indirect, such as suggesting a business deal. It might be done socially or through an activity like a game of tennis. In most instances, he would be approached by a person claiming to be someone other than who he really was. The purpose would be to build a bridge of trust before going further. At some point the case officer would reveal his own identity and convince the person that his special services were needed.

The interesting part of my situation was that I recognized every step of the process. I knew my case officers, Ken White and Danny Ishida, must take one final step. They must develop me or train me to work with them in a certain specific way before I could be relied upon to perform in the big maneuver, so I asked them what it was they wanted me to do.

They told me that initially they'd like me to perform a simple courier function. I could understand that. It was a very logical request. Businessmen are often asked to carry messages or packages for the intelligence services, a method less secure but more difficult to track than the traditional diplomatic pouches.

More significantly I realized they were embarking on a training process to develop me and to determine my reliability. Hopefully this would imbue me with a desire to perform precisely and loyally. I'd done this as a case officer with my own agents dozens of times. Developing an agent is the process of getting him accustomed to his meetings with his case officer and honing his reliability to the exact minute of punctuality.

If I were developing (training) an agent, I would approach the task methodically. I would ask him to meet me in front of a certain store, next to a certain green garbage can, and exchange newspapers with me in a certain way. Although there's no information or other significance to these two newspapers (it's just a training exercise), the agent must perform precisely to the minute in order to qualify for the next step. White and Ishida were using the same process to develop me over the next twelve months.

I did present a special challenge to White and Ishida, however. Because I knew these steps so well, I could have easily pretended the correct role and led them to believe I actually was being controlled by my case officers. So I had the extra challenge of convincing them I was for real and thus earn their trust.

No pay was offered or expected, but my expenses would be fully covered. My first task or training exercise was to carry a sealed letter and have it delivered to an address in San Francisco. Several more mail drops were carried out that first year, in September and December of 1981, and April of 1982.

In July of 1982, the game plan was suddenly changed. Exactly one year from our first meeting, Ken White and Danny Ishida came to me in my Tokyo hotel room and announced a major change in the project. Ken White said, "Craig, San Francisco did not come out to play." I knew precisely what he meant.

In order to clarify the meaning of Ken's comment, I must explain that my very first courier-drop was a sealed letter to be taken to an address in San Francisco.

My specific instructions, at the time of my first meeting with Ken White exactly one year before, were to:

1. Place in my briefcase a certain typed message that he would give me
2. Take a plane to Los Angeles, upon my return to the U.S.
3. Get to a "safe" typewriter in the Los Angeles area
4. Retype the message in letter-form in my own style and wording without altering its meaning
5. Destroy the old text
6. Make a copy of the new letter to give to White and Ishida next time we met in Tokyo
7. Take a plane to San Francisco
8. Go to a certain bonded public courier
9. Place the new letter in their regular envelope
10. Address it to the San Francisco Soviet Consulate
11. Prepay the courier to deliver it there

The text of this letter to the Soviets was an anonymous offer to give them information "on robotics and other high-tech matters." They were to respond by placing a classified ad in a certain newspaper.

I was already aware that they hadn't responded because I made it a point to check that paper's ads periodically. I was reasonably sure the other drops were strictly training drops into the nearest U.S. mail slot whenever I arrived in the U.S. from Tokyo.

Thus Plan A, an attempt by courier to lure the Soviets into conversations with a nameless American businessman, had not been successful. The lack of a response was no surprise because the Soviet consulates in the U.S. are far more cautious than are those abroad.

Plan B was next. Ken said, "I know that in the beginning we told you you'd only be involved as a courier, but having gotten no response, we feel that some kind of a direct approach to a Soviet installation here in Tokyo is indicated." He continued, "Because of your travels and your prior experience, we need your help. We need your ideas. Will you help us?"

Ken paused for a moment, but before I could reply he said, "For instance, take Operation (classified name). You were the case officer on that one. Do you feel that we could use the same combination of courier drop and walk-in approach you used in that operation?"

This operation was in a U.S. city that I cannot name, but the method of operation had some possibilities. I recommended a couple of significant changes, and we talked for a half-hour or more about where, when, and especially how to get them to invite us in.

When we finally got to who, Ken got very quiet. He leaned forward in his chair, and said, "Craig, would you agree to make a walk-in approach to the commercial office of the Soviet Embassy?"

He went on. "What I'm really asking you to do is to pretend to be a disloyal American—a disaffected former intelligence officer—and offer to sell them information."

I agreed to discuss this scenario further with them. But I told them I did not want a long relationship with them because of my commitment to my wife and family.

Ken White said, "Craig, let me explain it to you this way. You would only be a sort of hook, and the information you would offer would be the bait. We'd pull you out then, and another agent would take over."

The information Ken referred to, by the way, was data the Soviets already had. Why give them old news? Simply so they could check it out and attach credibility to their newly acquired source.

I was not told specifically what their long-range objective was, but it seemed certain they wanted to expose someone fairly high up in the San Francisco Soviet Consulate as a KGB spy.

Before they would discuss any further details of the case, I was asked to sign a new security agreement which obligated me to absolute secrecy. It was again a standard procedure and a familiar form. It even went so far as to have you agree to notify them if you are ever to be anesthetized for surgery, so they could be present.

At this point in our discussions, it occurred to me that the safe and easy tasks were over, and that if I agreed to this next and final step, I would be taking a much more significant risk—perhaps the greatest I had ever taken in the intelligence business.

I was to be inside the Soviet compound offering to sell the Russians U.S. government secrets while pretending to be a traitor. If they were to catch me in this delusion, I might as well be in Siberia because, in international law, embassy compounds are the same as foreign soil.

If I were caught, they could simply expose me and throw me out on the street. They could arrest me and deport me to Moscow for trial or they could kill me on the spot. Finally, if I were caught, the CIA wouldn't know me—they'd deny any involvement. No cavalry would ride in and rescue me. And for all this, no pay—just expenses. Anyone in his right mind would run the other way.

Why did I even consider it? The answer to this question is really quite simple. I *could* pull it off, and I *should* pull it off.

Obviously the assessment phase of the CIA's recruitment process told them that I *could* successfully accomplish the task, and my own experience told me the same thing. In fact, not too many former members of the intelligence community fit their "profile for success" in this operation. That is why, as soon as the major mission was revealed, I finally realized why they chose me to be their recruit.

The only negative on the "I could" side was Susan, who could not be told that I was involved in any way with an espionage operation. This weighed heavily on my mind as I pondered my decision.

I faced the final question, why *should* I?

My country has always ranked right up with my family and my

church in importance to me. There was a need. There was an opportunity. I felt it was my patriotic duty to serve when called. After all, this is how we're trained in our schools and churches and in our communities; we serve when called.

Frankly, it never even occurred to me to question a call from my country. I didn't really consider it a choice which was mine to make. If Susan eventually found out that I was working again, she was strong enough to understand why.

I said to Ken White and Danny Ishida, "Okay, let's get started!" We sat down and picked a date for the walk-in penetration, in November, just three-and-a-half months away.

At the end of the meeting, when Ken said goodbye and went to the door, he added, "Craig, just one more thing. You know how the game is played. If you're discovered or exposed by the Soviets, by the Japanese police, by the press of any country—by anyone—the Agency will disavow you. Good luck!"

5

A New Business Career

There is a reason I had returned to Japan.

In September of 1979, when Mike Davis and I sat in a tent in a meadow of the High Uinta Mountains planning our new life as civilians, the conversation centered around going back to Salt Lake City and getting back into the mainstream of life there—getting back in touch with our childhood joys and passing them on to our children.

I told him of my maternal grandmother, Augusta Monson, who had died in her nineties a year earlier. I told him how her great gift of a warm sense of humor and a steady faith in God's plan for mankind had inspired her children and grandchildren to live upright, positive lives. It was a shame that our own children and grandchildren couldn't have heard that special smile in her voice and seen that twinkle in her eyes.

I'd heard of a new video-will service offered by a law firm in Los Angeles. Wouldn't a video-journal be even more important? It would span the years of time down through the generations with a live hour of conversation with a beloved grandparent. When I asked my own father just how much he'd be willing to pay for such a video of his own father, tears welled up in his eyes because his father had died shortly after he was born.

"There's no price that could ever be attached to such a document," he said.

Thus the Timespan Corporation was born. Mike and I moved our families to adjacent areas in North Salt Lake City, and our business was launched. Timespan conducted professional interviews with family members, we also video-taped weddings and anniversaries.

We had achieved our first goal, that of getting back to our roots, with this amazing new medium of video-recording. Others may disagree, but we felt the Lord had given this new technology to his children, and we were determined to use it for some good purpose other than just making soap commercials.

It soon became apparent, however, that we had two major problems, one which might have been avoidable and one that was probably inevitable.

First, we underestimated our start-up costs. We didn't realize how much capital it would take to market a new concept in a very conservative community. Ideas like this were easier to sell in California where both of us had been living.

Secondly, we had launched Timespan just before the great breakthroughs in video-recording technology. VCR's and video-cameras had been too costly and complicated for the average person. Suddenly, they were available to the mass market and were simple to use as well. "One-button" simplicity made them easy to operate, and the cost came tumbling down so that people could buy the equipment and record their own interviews for little more than we were having to charge to cover our expenses.

Consequently, in 1981, we were forced to shift our marketing to the commercial and industrial sector and begin to film documentaries and trade show programs for businesses and entire industries. We were very successful, especially in the area of foreign trade. My overseas experience and language capabilities helped us get started.

For one such project, we flew a small crew to Bolivia and produced three documentary programs for the Utah-Bolivia Partners, a member of the National Partners of the Americas. These programs had to do with community education, community health, and cultural exchanges between the State of Utah and sister groups in the high plains villages of Bolivia.

We organized a state-endorsed trade mission to Japan in which twelve Utah-based companies participated. We produced a twelve-segment corporate brochure for showing in Tokyo and Osaka. In this format the companies' representatives could not only go in person and explain their programs, they also could take their factory with them and walk the viewers through the plant on video-tape rather than having to fly Japanese investors to Utah.

That was when interest rates rose to an all-time high, and U.S. companies were aggressively seeking off-shore investment capital, especially from countries like Japan where interest rates were still in the single digit range.

In order to organize a trade mission like this, we had to have our target audience lined up well in advance, so I went to Tokyo in June and again in July of 1981. It was during this second trip that the two CIA agents called on me at my Tokyo hotel room.

In order to reach the right audience, doors must be opened, so I started with the American Trade Center and the Commercial Section of the U.S. Embassy in Tokyo on my first visit in June. They advised me to get a businessman's representative, one of a number of Americans who lived in Japan, to invite the right people from various sectors of business and government to attend an advance briefing and later, the trade mission itself.

I knew a representative by the name of Tony DeGrasse from a previous venture, and when I returned in July it was obvious Tony had been busy. All the people I'd asked him to invite—plus a few others —were there. When Ken White called me on the phone, I simply assumed he'd been contacted directly or indirectly by Tony and was calling to catch up on our program.

The trade mission that was held in two Japanese cities in October of 1981 was very well received. We were invited by a Japanese government agency, JETRO: Japanese External Trade Organization, to repeat it in the Los Angeles area for Japanese businessmen in the U.S. I made many trips to Japan during 1981 to promote the upcoming trade mission and to follow up on leads developed thereby.

It was during these trips in 1981 and 1982 that I met with Ken White and/or Danny Ishida five or six times, and I had a number of telephone conversations with them.

Our success in Japan led to plans for similar trade missions by companies in California and Florida, especially medical high-tech firms. We had even negotiated for the participation of Dr. Robert Jarvik. He might go with us to discuss the famous artificial heart he'd been working on for some years. He would have been a real drawing card.

We also attracted the attention of a major nationwide real estate firm that wanted to show properties to potential investors in Japan, Taiwan, and Hong Kong, along with our high-tech trade shows.

All of this was very expensive to put together, and even though we'd made money with our first Utah show, we had to have a financial success this next time to survive.

Such was not to be, and it was only a matter of adverse timing. Dr. Jarvik and his medical team were not allowed to try their first heart implant until December of 1982, which was too late for us to wait. The real estate project fell apart when our client was purchased by another giant company, and this changed their game plan.

By the end of 1982, Timespan was in a serious cash flow situation, and we filed for reorganization under chapter eleven late that year. We could have attracted additional capital from our own investors in early 1983, but the board of directors decided against taking that risk and closed the company. We filed for both corporate and personal bankruptcy early in 1983, and we decided I would to go back to college in the fall of 1983 to finish a degree in communication.

Meanwhile, the other life I was living for the CIA was building to a crescendo.

6

The First CIA Mission to Tokyo

It was my eighth trip to Japan in the fourteen months that Timespan had been working toward sending trade missions to the Far East, and it was the fifth meeting with Ken White and Danny Ishida. The date was July 28th, 1982.

I'd been performing courier functions for exactly one year when Ken White suddenly changed the game plan and asked me to do a walk-in approach to the Soviet Embassy in Tokyo.

We were in my room in Tokyo in the New Otani Hotel discussing the details of this attempt at making a deep incursion into the KGB, and I had agreed to go ahead. They asked me to sign a security agreement in which I promised not to disclose the details of this operation. Then they laid out the plan in general form, and we began together to work out those details.

When an operation like this is planned, someone higher up lays out the basics, someone who has the big picture in mind. The case officers then fine-tune the details with the agent. For example, the agent cannot use a key word or sentence not in keeping with his own personality or vocabulary, so many of Ken White's suggestions had to be discussed and refined, a process known as "massaging the scenario."

Here is a case in point. The original plan called for me to go to a pay phone—phone calls are never made from a traceable source like a hotel room—and call the Soviet Embassy first. I suggested calling Tass, the Soviet News Agency first, to arrange a meeting with the Russians, for two reasons. First, it would tend to authenticate my claim to being a former intelligence officer because it would show that I knew that the Tokyo office of Tass was manned by a KGB officer. As head of Tass and as a member of the foreign press, this correspondent had far more freedom to travel than did other people in the Soviet Embassy. Second, the Tass person would call the embassy, probably at a higher level than I could reach, and alert them that I might be calling to "do business." The embassy people would more readily believe their man at Tass than they would a cold call from me. Ken agreed.

But another case in point went the other way. I was asked to build my case to the Soviets around medical problems, suggesting that I had terminal cancer and had no insurance or savings for my family. This would justify my motive to defect and sell secrets for cash.

I strenuously resisted this proposal as I felt I could develop enough motivation without risking a scenario so far from the truth. The best cover story is only slightly different from the truth, and this proposed medical situation was too abstract and had no support in fact. The truth is that it proved to be a mistake and might have gotten me killed. However, Ken was adamant and the medical scenario stuck.

Next we worked out a timetable allocating three days beginning November 5, 1982, for this attempt to walk in. My associates and family wouldn't know where I was.

We planned the approach around a trip when I would be scheduled to be in Tokyo with Utah's then Lt. Governor, later congressman, David Monson, on new development and follow-up calls to attract medical high-tech investments in Utah. David was to go on to a government meeting in Taipei, Taiwan, that wouldn't involve me, so I was to catch up with him three or four days later in Taipei.

Meanwhile, our Japanese contacts all assumed I had left Tokyo with the Lt. Governor.

Thus I was free to work the operation for three days because it's never known in advance how long a project like this might take. Perhaps no one could see me the first day.

There were some interesting facets of this planning process. I sensed that my depth of experience was somewhat greater than Ken White's, so my suggestions were taken seriously and, for the most part, adopted. Contrast this with the intense level of commitment I had developed toward my case officer even though I knew the development process backward and forward. I knew my loyalty to my case officer would pay off—possibly even save my life.

The die was now cast. The stage was set. On the appointed day, I stepped to a pay phone in Shinjuku and called the number listed for Tass. A Japanese woman answered first and told me to wait, then a man's voice answered.

I said, "I'm an American businessman in Tokyo, and I have information that I think would be of interest to the Soviet government, information about robotics and other technology matters. I would like to meet with somebody to discuss a proposal that may be of value to you."

"What kind of information are you talking about specifically?" the Tass man asked.

"It's something that must be discussed confidentially," I answered.

"Well we don't handle anything like that," he said. "Why don't you call the Soviet Embassy?"

This was exactly the exchange of conversation we'd hoped for, because it meant that Tass would preannounce my next phone call, and I could legitimately say, "I was told by the Tass representative to call the Embassy."

It was important that I wait about twenty minutes to allow the embassy to get the word up to the highest level that there was a possible walk-in about to phone them. If I hadn't used this approach, it's possible that a direct phone call would have resulted in the assessment that my call was some kind of provocation, and the orders would have been to "get that guy out of here as soon as he comes to the gate!"

Also, twenty minutes gave them time to line up the right security officer to handle the call, someone high up the ladder. Plus—and we smile at this—it gave them time to be sure their wire taps and voice recorders were in place.

As it turned out, I realized that they hadn't been quite ready because when I phoned the embassy, I was cut off and had to dial a second time. Maybe they were still splicing wires. But on the second call, I stated my interests exactly as I had to Tass, and a man answered, "Yes, we would be interested in talking to you."

It is important to understand that in order to establish credibility, Ken and Danny and I had built into our scenario a number of "outs" for the Russians. If you give them "outs," built-in escapes to get out of it, they feel safer coming in. If they're pushed, however, they usually become even more suspicious, so you give them exit opportunities.

It was for this reason I said to the man on the embassy phone, "If you're interested in this, call me back at the La Scala Coffee Shop in fifteen minutes. Here's the phone number."

They were given the opportunity not to call. They could just wash their hands and walk away. It also gave our side a chance to test them, to see how committed they were, how excited they were by whether or not they called back, and whether they called on time or not. In effect, we were beginning to train them, to control them, to get them to respond to us—much like a case officer trains and controls his agent. It's hard to believe, but it's true.

They called the coffee shop phone right on schedule. We knew then that there was a high degree of interest. They said, "Yes, we'd be very interested in meeting with you. Why don't you come over to the commercial compound (of the Soviet Embassy)?"

La Scala Coffee Shop, Tokyo, Japan.

I said, "No, I can't meet you there. I'd like to meet some place outside of the commercial compound." It wasn't because I was not willing to go in there. Of course I wanted to go in—that was the goal. If I were to go in and claim to be a former intelligence officer, it would be out of character and suspiciously naive to go in so readily and to make it so easy to get me inside. They should have to work at getting me in.

I said, "I'll meet you outside. Let's meet at a restaurant or a hotel or someplace that will be safe for both of us."

They continued to ask me to "come over," but finally we compromised by agreeing to have them call for me in the lobby of the Takanawa Tobu Hotel, which was adjacent to the commercial compound.

It was a matter of getting a little bit closer together. "I'll come this far, if you'll come that far," or, "I'll come next door, if you'll call me when I get there, and then, when we're only a hundred yards apart, we'll see where we go from there." Thus we kept giving them "outs," and yet we kept building into them the perception that they were giving us "outs" too, but we kept coming.

The Takanawa Tobu Hotel, Tokyo, Japan.

I sat in the lobby of the designated hotel and waited for their call. To this point the scenario was running exactly as planned through the first three phone calls. From there forward, I was on my own because we couldn't have predicted exactly where the next phone call would lead.

I knew, however, that I was being tailed by our own CIA people just as Ken and Danny had promised. They wanted to "backstop" me all the way into the embassy compound, which was very reassuring, if for no other reason than the fact that it proved that the CIA really was in charge of this operation. I also knew, without being told, that if anything went wrong, the sheriff's posse wouldn't ride in and save me.

As the operation moved ahead into uncharted waters, I left spaces of time for this backup surveillance to catch up with me, and I observed them as they took up their new positions outside the hotel.

The phone call came about fifteen minutes late, but the fact that it did come meant they were probably scrambling to get their own surveillance people placed in readiness to receive me inside the compound. It was the same voice as the last call—later identified as that of Viktor I. Okunev, one of the highest KGB officers in the Far East, the man I would meet and deal with.

Okunev said, "All right, if you want us to cooperate, you'll have to come inside the compound. You're the person making the proposal. We're willing to listen, but if you want to talk to us, you must come over."

I've been asked if I thought his calls were being monitored by either the CIA or the Japanese police. I don't know. I must point out, though, that both of us took care to speak "generically." I spoke originally of ideas about technology and robotics. He spoke of interest, but nothing that would point to classified areas or the specifics of sensitive information—yet. That could only come later, when we were talking inside. Now we were exactly where we wanted to be, so after some staged resistance, I agreed to take the next step.

I left the hotel and walked about a block and a half away from the compound. I had to assume at this point that they knew who I was because they had designated the phone contact point. I knew that we now would have not only my own people following me, we would have their people as well. If I were to go in and tell them I was a former intelligence officer, I would have had to show them more class than to walk straight to the compound.

Thus I walked down to the train station, bought a ticket, and came back out again. I picked up my own coverage easily, but I never did see theirs. (Frankly, our people aren't always very good.)

Soviet Embassy commercial compound gate, Tokyo, Japan.

This time I walked straight to the gate of the Soviet Embassy's commercial compound. At this point an interesting question must be asked. If I truly had committed treason by acting on my own to sell secrets to the Soviets, would I have walked straight up to that gate, knowing as I did that both sides were tailing me and that both sides have elaborate hidden cameras focused on that gate night and day? It would have been suicide!

I pressed the buzzer. It had been about ten minutes since the last phone call. The electronic gate opened. I walked into a large courtyard and saw two buildings, but there was no indication as to which I should enter. The door was locked on one so I entered the other, which looked more like a dormitory. I climbed a small service stairway, walked around, and returned by another stairway.

I was amazed at the access I had to the building and wondered if I had been mistaken for a resident of the compound and was not being monitored at all.

Finally I came to the basement floor and eventually saw someone at the far end of the hallway. As I walked toward him, windows along the hall revealed all manner of controls and TV monitors. Obviously I was approaching the duty office of the compound. What I could have shot with a camera! Certainly by now I was being videotaped.

I'd spent about ten minutes exploring the back hallways of the Soviet Embassy when I finally met two very embarrassed Russian officers in front of their embassy's nerve center. I think they mistook me on the gate camera for one of their own people and were still waiting for the real me to appear. It's even possible that I shook them off when I doubled back to the train station, and they accidentally passed me in while discussing the probability that I'd decided against meeting them after all. I walked up to one of them and said, "I'm David. I spoke to you on the phone."

It was Okunev himself. He'd paged me as "Mr. David" at the hotel by prearrangement. For just a moment there was an expression of surprise and confusion on his face. Then he edged me away from the windows, down a hall to a darkened lobby and into a chair.

"What can we do for you?" he asked in perfect English, with a slight Russian accent.

If I chose to, I could now paint a dramatic, suspense-filled picture for you of nerves and fright and tension—of walking into what could easily have been my last look at freedom or even life itself. In truth, it was almost comic opera. At the least, it was about as routine as any visit to an unknown office in a strange building. In spite of the high risk, I was calm and composed, observing and measuring as best I could the details of what was happening.

Finally, I spoke again. "You're the gentleman I spoke to on the phone, aren't you?"

"Yes, I am."

"Well, I'm an American businessman, and a former Army intelligence officer. I can prove to you that I was an intelligence officer, and I am currently dealing with companies involved with high-tech robotics. I could give you certain information that would be of interest to your government."

I told him that my motives were purely for the financial security of my family, and that no ideology was involved.

I said, "I'm sick. I may not be around very long, and I want to make sure that my family is financially secure." Then I said, "I'll prove that I am who I say I am, and that I have the access I say I have, but I won't give you the information I'm speaking of until you're satisfied I'm authentic."

I followed the scenario rehearsed with Ken White and Danny Ishida right to the letter. As we had agreed also, I gave no hint as to my real name in the event we wanted to scrub the mission after this first contact.

Okunev asked, "What is your real name? Do you have any identification?"

I'd left my ID in a secure place, so I said, "It really doesn't matter until we reach some sort of agreement."

He accepted that and said, "Okay."

Then I said, "This is my proposal: I will prove to you that I am who I say I am and I will give you information, but I want $25,000."

This was the sum agreed upon with Ken White. I strongly concurred because it wasn't an outrageous amount of money, yet it was more than the Soviets like to pay initially.

On the other hand, if I had been on my own for illegal espionage (treason) I would never have met them on their turf, and I would have asked for no less than $150,000—one time only—and never gone back. It was just too foolish and dangerous.

I then gave Okunev a few bits and pieces of the intelligence picture in Japan which the CIA told me to use for bait—just enough so the Soviets could authenticate me.

After I made my proposal, Okunev said, "We are very interested in your proposition. I think it can be arranged, but I'll have to get approval from my superiors. How can I get in touch with you?

I knew they were reaching for any additional information about me they could possibly get. I asked him, "How long will it take to get an answer?"

He said, "Probably a day or two."

I allowed three days. It usually takes a day or two to check out information like the preplanned tidbits I gave him.

I then said, "Well, if you want to reach me, if the answer you get from your superiors is a positive answer, and you're interested in this proposal, then call me and page me day after tomorrow at twelve noon in the lobby of the Keio Plaza Hotel in Shinjuku."

Of course, this was not the hotel where I stayed.

"You can page 'Mr. David,' " I added.

He said, "No, let's not use 'Mr. David' this time." Obviously he knew it was possible the previous "Mr. David" conversation could have somehow been monitored. "This time, let's use the name 'Hemingway,' " he said.

"All right," I agreed, "Page 'David Hemingway' at precisely twelve o'clock noon. I'll pick up the page, and you can tell me where to meet you."

We shook hands, left the room, and he took me to his car. He pulled the visors down and asked me to slouch down low in the rear seat. Since the windows were quite dark anyway, surveillance eyes or cameras would probably not see me inside.

They drove me through what we call a dry cleaning process for about fifteen minutes to make sure we weren't being followed and finally dropped me off in a residential neighborhood.

Of course it occurred to me that their own prearranged surveillance could have picked me up at this point, so I did my own dry cleaning with a couple of cabs. When I knew I was clean, I picked up my ID and other belongings from a public locker and returned to my motel to wait for a couple of days to pass.

On the second day I went to the Keio Plaza Hotel and waited for the call. Sure enough it came, at straight-up twelve noon. There was a humorous twist. The page wasn't for "Mr. Hemingway," it was for "Mr. Shakespeare." I told the desk clerk I was "David Shakespeare" and took the house phone.

I recognized the voice and told Okunev, "I think you got the names mixed up."

He laughed, and said, "Yes, I thought about that, just after I gave the name to the hotel operator. I'm glad you picked up the page, anyway."

Okunev and I laughed about this incident later on. Other than my first entrance to the embassy, I think this was the only technical mistake he ever made.

He said to me, "My superiors have agreed to your proposal." He told me he wanted to meet me inside the compound again that evening. I agreed to be there.

I was a little surprised that I was to walk back in. Was this another technical mistake? Anyway, this was the last walk-in. The next time they picked me up at a neutral location and took me in the car, slumped down in the back seat with a hat pulled down low.

This second meeting was held in a carefully prepared room, laid out with delicious hors d'oeuvres, soft drinks, beer, and vodka available—with obvious camera and sound equipment in place.

Okunev had a list of questions, and I answered those I was authorized to answer. The rest I did not. I gave them only about one-third of the information I was authorized to give them, just a little more information than they already had to enable them to check me out further and whet their appetite for more.

At the end of this session, Okunev gave me a small brown envelope containing $5,000—fifty one-hundred-dollar bills. I slipped the envelope into my inside coat pocket.

We arranged to meet again in February of 1983, but no date was set. Instead, he gave me a confidential phone number I could call clandestinely.

One of the objectives of this CIA operation was to get to a certain key officer of the KGB in the San Francisco Soviet Consulate. The first step was somehow to get that consulate to become involved in contacting me, to let them know they had a new player in town, to start building a bridge over to me, and eventually, hopefully, invite me in for discussions.

For this reason, and according to the scenario, I got a bit brash with Okunev and told him to have his San Francisco people page me in the lobby of the St. Francis Hotel at exactly twelve noon on December 18, 1982, and to instruct them to pay me the balance of the $25,000 in San Francisco.

Of course it was not the money that was of major concern; we just wanted to force some kind—any kind—of participation on the part of the Soviet Consulate in San Francisco.

The meeting ended and they took me out, as usual, in the dark-windowed car. I took the usual precautions to be sure I wasn't followed to my hotel. Then I left for Taipei the next morning to catch up with Lt. Gov. Monson.

I've been asked why I didn't report to Ken or Danny immediately, or at least before leaving Tokyo, about these extraordinarily successful penetrations into the KGB. The reason is simple. One of the first things the Soviets look for is an immediate report to a superior. Many good operations have been compromised that way. It used to be that agents would walk out of a meeting, do three minutes worth of dry cleaning and then, get on the phone and say, "I'm out. I'm done." In fact, they were still being watched.

It's far safer to go right on with your normal routine for a day or two and then call your case officer. In this case, I waited until I was back in Salt Lake City, went to a pay phone, and dialed what we call a "hello phone" number that Ken White had set up. He got my message from the person in Honolulu taking his calls, and then it was his turn to step to a pay phone in Tokyo, Honolulu, or wherever and call me at my office.

To protect these conversations about events so sensitive and secret, a kind of double-speak known in the intelligence community as "open-text code" is used. Thus we sound like any two businessmen talking things over.

I could be sitting in the comfort of my own office, getting a call from Tokyo, and saying, "I met with our client, and he approved our contract." This is exactly how we talk.

In this case, I said, "We have a deposit, and one of his representatives is going to be in San Francisco in December, and I'm going to be having a conversation with them then about some additional funding for the project. I'm probably looking at going back over in January or February to actually execute the contract."

Then Ken White replied something like this: "Well, how much of a deposit did you get?"

I said, "Well, I got $5,000 down, and there may be some additional expenses covered in December."

It's a prearranged code. Anyone sitting right in my office would not have any idea we weren't talking routine business. Ken asked, "Did you have any problems? Do you anticipate any further difficulties?

I replied, "No, everything went smoothly and according to the business plan."

* * * * *

There was a tremendous feeling of exhilaration and satisfaction throughout the episode with the Russians, then and immediately thereafter. Perhaps I was a little afraid that the operation might fail, but I did not experience fear. I could feel the adrenalin, of course, but I wasn't nervous.

I didn't do this for my own ego. I did it out of duty to my country.

One might consider an analogy. When someone gives a kidney to a loved one, does he do it for his own ego? Of course not. He does it because he loves that person and there's a critical need. It was exactly like that in my own case. I had a skill to give, and the country that I love had a critical need. Under the same circumstances, there's no question that I would do it again.

I must comment on the satisfaction I gained from achieving even more than I ever dreamed I could in this operation.

Case officers have excellent people working as agents for them, but they never go directly into the action themselves. Each of us, however, is positive that he would be a better agent than his own very best people in the field.

I had finally gotten the chance to prove what I always felt I could do, given the opportunity.

The most intriguing question was: now that the toughest door in the world had been cracked open, how would my country take the best advantage of it?

7

My Wife Susan

It's important to remember that when I left the intelligence business, I did so for my wife and children. In the final analysis, I left for my own good because my family was and is number one. I had told Susan I'd never work in intelligence again, and she believed me.

It was enormously difficult to keep my new secret from her. Yet I had to in order to insure the success of the operation and to stay alive myself. It's one thing to be in the spy business and have a wife and family who know you can't tell them anything, but it's another matter to get back into the business secretly, without their knowledge or approval.

From the day of our wedding in 1972, until I left the government in January of 1980, Susan knew exactly what I did for a living. She just didn't know any of the details. She knew that this work was extremely important to me.

She also developed an acute sense of how I behaved under different degrees of stress. For example, during the first year of our marriage I was in language school, so there was no particular pressure on me then. Even the first six months in Japan there wasn't any great stress. Then I moved into a more sensitive area in my training to become a case officer, and it began to be apparent to Susan that I was under significantly more pressure. She could detect this just by continual observation.

Thereafter, whenever I went into an "operational mode," she sensed it because she was so tuned-in to my behavior. There was a very slight shift in my personality when I had a case going forward, and Susan was able to see this in me.

I became more intense and reclusive, not nervous, just quicker to tire, and less patient. Like any husband and wife, we learned to spot these sudden shifts in each other's attitudes.

When I was actively involved (we call it "working") she knew it. She had developed the ability to know because of her prior conditioning.

When I left the government in 1980, my personality changed in many ways. All of that pressure, duplicity, and everything else that had been a part of our lives for so long was gone, and we were incredibly happy that first year. It was the first time we'd really been able to share ourselves with each other from the day we'd been married.

When the CIA recruited me in 1981, my first year with the Agency had placed no serious pressures on me—just minor tasks like letter drops to complete my training. Susan really didn't notice any change in me.

In 1982, however, when Ken and Danny changed the game plan and we began preparing for my meeting with the Soviets, the pressure began to mount. I was operating on the inside now. I was literally back in business.

There obviously was a shift then, and Susan noticed that there was a change in me. I don't believe she suspected that I was working again, but she knew something was wrong. She attributed it to the fact that the business was experiencing some difficulties, and she assumed that pressures of the office were causing the change in my behavior. She never really came out and said she suspected anything.

It was only when I took Susan to Honolulu with me that she began to suspect the real thing. I'd arranged to meet Ken White in Honolulu for a deferred debriefing in January of 1983, two months after I met Okunev in Tokyo.

This time I had no excuse to be in Hawaii, so I talked a travel agency who was a client of ours into my shooting some commercial footage for them in Waikiki; that way I'd have a reason to be there.

Ironically, Susan almost spoiled my cover trip. When she heard I was going on business, not wanting me to enjoy the sun and beach alone, she said, "Please, honey, take me with you."

To salvage the situation, I told my younger brother Todd, who knew nothing of my activities either, to take his wife Becky and come along also. Susan would thus have company while I met with Ken.

So we went with a two-man camera crew, and I arranged a meeting with Ken at two-thirty one afternoon. Since I had no other business in Honolulu, I had to leave the group on some kind of flimsy excuse, promising to be back by five for dinner.

The Westin Ilikai Hotel, Waikiki, Honolulu, Hawaii. Photo by Westin Ilikai.

I went to the Ilikai Hotel in Waikiki, where Ken and I met at "The Top of the I," because no one would be at the penthouse restaurant in mid-afternoon. We went back down to the street and took Ken's car to a small restaurant near the park at the other end of Waikiki Beach. There I underwent an intensive debriefing of my November meetings with Okunev and was briefed for my February meeting.

By the time Ken dropped me back at our hotel, it was well after five. Given her sensitivity to me, Susan could hardly fail to note that first, I was late, second, I had no alibi—no place I could logically have been—and third, I had just come from a very intensive intelligence debriefing. I was indeed working. When I tried to make the transition from the debriefing mode to the let's-stroll-out-and-have-dinner mode, Susan became suspicious.

She gave me a little flack about being late, and then as we fell back a few paces from the others, she said, "You're working, aren't you?"

I replied, "What do you mean?" I wasn't about to lie to her if I could help it.

She said, "If I didn't know better, I'd think you were back in the business."

I didn't actually deny it, but I passed it off and changed the subject. However, I knew it was just a matter of time until I'd have to level with her. It wasn't until a whole year had gone by that I was actually forced to tell Susan that I'd gone back into spying—this time for the CIA.

Before this happened, we went through many trying, confusing and moments. As each flag went up and she noticed more pressure and tension mounting within me, she'd ask me questions. For example, she'd ask, "What's wrong? Is it the business going bad that's causing you to act so distant?"

She'd ask the age-old questions millions of spouses have been forced to ask each other, "What's happening to our marriage? You just don't seem to be very interested in our marriage any more."

It was not that I wasn't interested. I was just preoccupied. I had a "mistress" relationship with my work that was mentioned earlier. This time it was worse than ever because even though she believed and hoped for the best, she was beginning to suspect the worst. My commitment to work for the CIA and my country was forcing me to hurt the one person I loved the most.

Perhaps it was a blessing in disguise when the FBI knocked on our door six months later and began a three-year ordeal which, although it completely disrupted our lives, forced me to break my secrecy and tell Susan the truth for the first time.

I was eight months into this three-year trial-by-fire when I finally told her the truth in February of 1984. I had just returned from my first Washington D.C. interview with the FBI, and I could keep my secret no longer.

I said, "Susan, I know that you've probably suspected that I've been working, and you're right. I have been—for the CIA. You've even asked about it a couple of times, and I've put off telling you the truth." I went on. "I need to tell you that for the past two-and-a-half years I've been working for the Agency, that we're involved in a very heavy operation, and that apparently something has gone terribly wrong. I don't know what it is yet, but I know that right now the FBI is looking at me, and they're investigating me.

"I want you to know that no matter what happens in this thing, I haven't done anything wrong, and the evidence will bear me out and prove me to be in the right."

For the next two or three days, it was very difficult for us even to speak to each other.

She supported me, however, and didn't back off. She said that she didn't like it and wished it had never happened. She also confirmed that she'd been almost certain I was working, from that incident in Waikiki onward.

I'm convinced that most wives would have gone straight to a lawyer at this point and filed for a divorce, but not Susan. Though I could never tell her, even though I still can't divulge all the details to her,

her loyalty has been absolute. Her courage has been strong. Her faith and trust in me will be an example and an inspiration to me and to our children for the rest of our lives.

Susan and Craig Smith.

8

The Second CIA Mission To Tokyo

During our second meeting in November, I had brazenly informed Okunev that if his side wanted to do further business, they would have to have their San Francisco people page me in the lobby of the St. Francis Hotel at exactly twelve noon on December 18th, 1982. They were to tell me, on the phone, how to collect the balance of my $25,000 in the United States if they expected me to deliver the rest of the information I had for them. The reason for this was to try to get San Francisco involved.

Consequently on Saturday, December 18th, I told Susan I had to go to the Timespan office in downtown Salt Lake City, and I did go there. Then I immediately left for the airport and took a plane to San Francisco, arriving in the lobby of the St. Francis at the appointed hour of twelve.

"Paging Mr. Walter Hamlin," the voice at the desk called out. That was my new paging name—Walter Hamlin. Okunev apparently tired of mixing up his authors.

I went to the nearest house phone and said, "This is Walter Hamlin."

The hotel operator said, "I have a call for you."

The Westin St. Francis Hotel, San Francisco, California. Photo by Westin St. Francis.

I waited, and a voice with a thick Soviet accent came on the line and said, "Mr. Hamlin, we accept your proposal, but we cannot do business in the U.S. You will have to go back to Tokyo."

I said, "No, that won't be possible. I can't go to Tokyo. We'll have to finish the transaction here in San Francisco."

Again, the prepared text: "Mr. Hamlin, we accept your proposal, but we cannot. . . ." It was obvious that he lacked either the authority or the English fluency to negotiate with me.

I got a little angry and replied, "No. That won't do. Our friend in Tokyo assured me that you would cooperate here on the paperwork."

I was using the same open-text code Ken and I used, but he just started reading again, "Mr. Hamlin, we accept your proposal, but. . . ."

I finally gave in and said, "Okay, I'll go to Tokyo."

We'd accomplished our main purpose. We'd forced San Francisco to come out and take some action, setting the stage for yet another step in the plan to penetrate the San Francisco Consulate. I walked out of the hotel delighted with the very real progress we were making. I caught a plane to Salt Lake City and returned home.

* * * * *

At nine o'clock Thursday morning, February 10th, 1983, I was in Tokyo. I left my room in the New Otani Hotel, went to a pay phone, and dialed a certain "beeper number" Okunev had given me at our last meeting in November. This would activate a beeper in the control room I'd accidentally discovered in the basement of the Soviet commercial compound. When I'd dialed three times, pausing a minute or two between, that signaled the Soviets to have Okunev meet me at the Miko Coffee Shop at exactly seven o'clock in the evening of the next day.

I went to the Miko, waited until two minutes past seven, and then left. Before Okunev or anyone else arrived, I realized that the coffee shop was closing at seven, so the meeting had to be aborted. My recontact instructions were that if no one showed the first evening, the meeting was automatically moved forward twenty-four hours. I returned the next evening on Saturday at seven o'clock to find the coffee shop already closed. Again we missed connections. I still could have been picked up by Okunev or his car, but after a minute I left again.

At this point, I was supposed to have started a new three-day cycle with the beeper, but I had to be in Taiwan and Hong Kong to meet David Monson. We had appointments scheduled for the following week.

The Miko Coffee Shop, Tokyo, Japan.

I shifted to Plan B, which was an emergency contact procedure. The next day Sunday, at 10:30 AM, I phoned the Soviet Embassy from a pay phone in a nearby subway station and asked for Mr. David. I was passed up a couple layers to some one who told me, "Mr. David is not here."

I said, "Then tell Mr. David that Mr. Hamlin will be at the hotel today only."

That meant he had to be found and taken to a pay phone in time to have me paged at the Keio Plaza Hotel at high noon, just an hour and a half from then.

Fortunately, the page came through on schedule, and it was Okunev. He said, "I apologize for not making the meetings. We did receive the beeper signal, but I couldn't meet you because of schedule conflicts."

I said, "Well are we going to meet or what?"

Okunev said, "Yes, let's meet tomorrow."

I said, "It will have to be tonight because I have a plane to catch."

My plane was actually for the next day, Monday, but I wanted to force a meeting on my terms again, so I said, "If we're going to meet, it will have to be tonight. Call me again at this hotel in exactly two hours. Meanwhile, I'll try to get on a later flight."

Of course, I'd have waited day after day for a week to have this next meeting, but it was threatening to conflict with my cover-trip to Taipei. Okunev did call back at two o'clock however, and I told him I'd changed my flight. We arranged to meet at the same coffee shop, but an hour earlier, at six o'clock that evening.

I arrived at precisely six o'clock and saw him inside. When he saw me approaching, he got up from his chair, met me at the door and led me down a couple of alleys to a street where we waited.

Since I had seen him last, he had grown a beard. He said he'd been to Moscow on my case.

Shortly his car pulled up, I was ushered into the rear seat and given the usual hat to wear. With visors down again, and behind dark glass windows, we started through dry cleaning, only this time at a very aggressive speed, as if a full-blown evasion of known surveillance was taking place. I never did find out the reason for it.

When we finally reached the compound gate, I got angry and said, "Okay, now look. This is the last time I'm coming to the compound. It's too dangerous to come here. We can meet in a hotel-room or any other place you want. We're in the compound this time, but it's the last time."

As a part of the plan, I hadn't eaten or slept much for three days in order to make my appearance of being ill look genuine. Apparently the dark circles under my eyes and my greasy, unwashed hair were convincing because Okunev remarked, "You don't look well."

I replied, "I don't feel well."

I felt apprehensive each time I entered the Soviet compound pretending to be dying of cancer, because if a doctor were called in to treat me, they could discover my ruse and I'd be history. What a price to pay for Ken White's insistence on the medical scenario. In all fairness to Ken White and Danny Ishida however, they were probably acting on higher orders to provide for the possibility the Agency might have to pull me out. I could claim that I was too sick to travel anymore, but the operation wouldn't have to be abandoned entirely.

I remembered the first time Okunev and I had met in the darkened lobby. He had said something that sent chills down my back. "We have excellent doctors in Moscow. We would be happy to make them available to you."

Now I wondered if he would bring up my "illness" this time and I determined that before I entered into Soviet territory again I would first have surgery, for no reason, just so I'd be able to produce a scar.

When Okunev and I were seated in the usual meeting room, I gave him information about two more operations of which I had detailed knowledge. Ken White had given me twelve different cases, which the Agency had authorized us to discuss with the Soviets. They'd all been terminated. They were all dead. They were finished. Some had never even developed into operations at all.

I remember that Ken had briefly shown me the list. Then holding it in his lap, he went over the operations one-by-one, asked, "What do you remember about this operation?"

We had discussed them one at a time. There were four operations where, even though my name appeared on the file, I really hadn't played a major role, so we scratched them. That left eight in which I had been directly involved as either case officer or alternate case officer. I'd given information concerning only four of these to Okunev at our second November meeting. There were four cases remaining for this current meeting, but I decided to reserve two of them in the event I needed more ammunition to keep the relationship alive.

The Agency had authorized me to give the Soviets only certain details of these specific operations, and I limited myself accordingly. When Okunev asked me for more details than those authorized, I simply said that I didn't know.

None of the details of these cases can yet be disclosed here because they're still classified. I can give you a hypothetical example. This is not actual, but it is similar to information I gave to Okunev about the cases that had been approved for this operation. "In 1973 we had a double agent operating in such and such country. Here was the agent's name, here was the code name of the operation, and here was the name of the Soviet case officer to whom he reported."

Of course the Soviets already knew all of this, but it would confirm that I too knew the details, and that was the part designed to convince the Soviets that I was real. Further, the fact that our side was involved in a double operation rendered this agent useless now to the Soviets anyway.

Here's another hypothetical example—this time of an operation which never actually occurred:

"In February of 19XX, in country Y, we put double agent Z on board Soviet cruise ship A between Port B and Port C. We 'dangled' him to try to get next to a particular Soviet officer on that ship who we knew was a KGB agent. We didn't succeed, and our agent left the ship at Port C."

The Soviets again would be able to check their files and verify that their man was the officer, that our man was on the passenger list, and that he did indeed travel only from Port B to Port C. A case which never happened is thus verifiable.

Again, none of this information was news to the Soviets. It merely enabled me to become more credible so that I'd be allowed deeper into their system. That was our plan.

It worked beautifully. In November, Okunev had asked, "Would you be willing to meet me in Vienna some time in the future?"

That was a stroke of fortune. He was one of the highest-ranking KGB officers ever to be compromised in recent U.S. espionage history. He was inviting me into the inner sanctum of Soviet espionage.

Vienna! Called the "City of Spies," probably more intelligence operations go on there than in any other city in the world. It's also the single most important city—anywhere—to Soviet Intelligence.

Vienna is the capital of a neutral country. It is adjacent to Eastern Europe, and since no one is spying on Austria, the live-and-let-live attitude of both the government and the tourist industry makes possible a lively espionage business.

I came away from my previous meeting surprised and delighted that I had convinced the Soviets that I was who I represented myself to be, a former Army Intelligence case officer, even though the four cases given to them to establish my credibility were already in their files. Nothing was new, but they were buying my future services, and that was exactly what we had wanted.

In my third meeting with Okunev in February, 1983, he brought up Vienna again, and we began setting specific dates for a future meeting with him in Vienna. We agreed to meet there during the second week of April, just two months later.

In our previous meeting, when Okunev asked me if I'd go to Vienna, he gave me three very important bits of information to help me make contact when I arrived.

He gave me an address in Vienna which was on Friedrichstrasse and a phone number which I was to dial. This would set off three "beeper" signals similar to those in Tokyo. Then I was to go by taxi to meet Okunev (or someone he delegated) at that certain address the next evening—again at seven o'clock. Thus Okunev began to reveal his "signature."

Almost every intelligence officer has a trusted "m. o." upon which he relies over and over, one method of contact, dead-drop, or other means of passing a message which begins to reveal his "pattern" or "signature." We can often identify the case officer who is managing an enemy agent just by his systems. It helps us set a trap, bait a hook, or arrange an intervention. It's a vital part of our objective in a double operation to get the decision maker to show his hand. Okunev, bright as he was, was beginning to show his.

Next he gave me the "parole" or "password" to authenticate myself if I were met by a stranger unknown to me. A "parole" is actually an authentication exchange, a verbal exchange between two agents. Literally, it means "the word." It generally consists of four exchanges, somewhat like the spoken lines of a play. The first two make sense with each other. For example, Okunev told me the person approaching me would ask, "Didn't I meet you in Paris in 1972?"

I was to answer, "No, I believe it was Rome."

Then he would say, "But it was '74, wasn't it?"

I would reply, "No, it was '76."

Not only would the second two fit each other, but they would stand for some detail in my personal life—in this case the birth years of my two middle children. However, the second pair would not fit the first pair, and thus an agent would avoid a coincidental exchange with the wrong person.

The one-week window was now set for our April meeting in Vienna, and I'd been given the contact details. There was only one last piece of business with Okunev before I was to be driven out in the darkened car again—my cash payment.

At our January meeting in Honolulu, Ken White had shown me a number of pictures of ranking KGB officials, and I had identified Okunev for the first time. His picture only identified him as a high officer in the KGB. It wasn't until well into our investigation, after my release from jail, that we discovered he was the third-highest ranked KGB officer in the Far East.

Since we did not yet have this detail, we needed to determine just how much authority Okunev had to make his own decisions in the field. Ken White's orders to me were to accept any sum he offered me, but to insist on exactly one thousand dollars more. The reason was to see if he was high enough in the KGB to have fairly wide latitude and operational authority to adjust his own game plan.

THE SECOND CIA MISSION TO TOKYO

When our meeting was at an end, Okunev produced a large manila envelope from his briefcase, and showed me what I estimated to be well over $50,000 U.S., plus perhaps $30,000 in Japanese yen. Then he said, "When you come to Vienna, if the information you bring us is as good as you've told us it will be, we're prepared to pay you $150,000 U.S."

He was careful to show me the extent of his fat pile of currency, no doubt thinking he would make sure he baited the hook. Instead, he had taken our bait—hook and all.

Then he produced just $5,000, placed it in a smaller envelope and handed it to me, putting the rest back into his case. I have no doubt I could have insisted on $5,000, $10,000, or even $15,000 more. After all, wasn't our initial agreement for $25,000? However, the money was of no consequence, and my orders were clear.

I said, "Say, you're pretty free with your money. That barely covers my travel just to come over here. Give me another thousand dollars." He did so, and I said goodbye and left by car again.

* * * * *

There are three crucial observations to be made at this point. First, reverse the picture for a moment. If I really were guilty of selling secrets to the Soviets, it would have been much simpler and safer to have met them in Vienna, gotten a transfer of $150,000 to a Swiss bank account, given them all they wanted, and then simply walked away for good. That would make more sense than going to the FBI and reporting receiving a mere $11,000 for three open trips in and out of the Soviet Embassy in Tokyo.

Secondly, after the second Okunev meeting in November, I began thinking of cover trips for both Tokyo in February and Vienna later on. Tokyo was easy; Timespan had many things going in Japan, Taiwan, and Hong Kong. I would have to concoct a similar mission to Europe from scratch, however.

Then, some time between the Okunev meetings in November and February, the Timespan phone rang in Salt Lake City, and the San Francisco Consul-General from Switzerland called me personally. He said, "I would like to come to Utah and meet with you about possibly organizing a trade mission similar to the one you held in Japan—from the state of Utah to Switzerland."

The ensuing news coverage of his visit to Salt Lake City, not to public officials but to Timespan and Craig Smith, provided the perfect cover for my trip to Europe. Coincidence? I'm sure it was, but when I told Okunev in February the details related above, he sort of smiled and showed no particular surprise.

The third observation to be made is that my last visit with Okunev left me with a peculiar sense of respect for my adversary. Of course, a thousand stories have been written of the dogmatic admiration of the hunter for his quarry. Okunev's patriotism probably equaled my own. His self-discipline and sense of timing no doubt brought him to his high level of command.

No one is certain of his whereabouts now. All we know is that he was immediately pulled out of the Far East when news of my arrest broke. We don't know his reaction, but I think I knew him fairly well, and I'm convinced he was shocked. He'd bought me ninety-eight per cent. Nobody in our business ever buys anyone one hundred per cent.

I don't know if he is alive.

9

The Spy Left Out In The Cold

Now the stage was truly set for what I'm convinced would have been one of the most significant penetrations of Soviet security in U.S. history.

It might be helpful to turn the picture around. When a ranking Soviet intelligence officer defects to the U.S., it's big news throughout all diplomatic, military, and intelligence communities; this has happened from time to time. Never has such a Soviet defector turned out to be a double agent however, in intimate and constant contact with his Soviet "handlers."

In fact, this was now the case with me. The Soviets were bringing me to Vienna to train me to work with them in what they thought was one of their major penetrations of all time of U.S. security.

It was imperative at this point that I make contact with Ken White, my case officer, and set up a debriefing of my last meeting with Okunev. Such a meeting would also get the authorization from the Agency for the Vienna trip in April, get a new batch of "feed" material and the authorization we needed to give it to the Soviets, and resolve the medical issue—to be able to produce a scar from a significant operation which apparently removed all malignant growths.

Accordingly, when I finally returned to Salt Lake City from the Far East, I dialed Ken's "hello phone" in Honolulu and waited for his return call. He called back five days later, and we scheduled a meeting in Honolulu during the first two weeks of March. As for the exact date, I had no reason to go to Honolulu again, so Ken said to get there as best I could during that time frame, dial again, and he'd come to a meeting.

When I arrived in Honolulu, I called Ken's phone immediately and waited for his call. The phone rang, but when I answered, it wasn't Ken!

A voice said, "This is Danny." I assumed it was Danny Ishida, although he'd spoken so seldom, I didn't have a strong recollection of his voice. He asked, "Do you know the stone footbridge in the Ala Moana Park?"

I answered, "Yes, of course."

"Meet me there at two o'clock tomorrow afternoon," he said, and hung up the phone.

I did the same, and the next day I went there as ordered. Soon a caucasian male approached and said, "I'm Dan."

I didn't even respond, as I was expecting Danny Ishida, the Japanese agent with the American accent. Then he flashed the same authenticator card shown me months earlier by Ken White. It was an ordinary business card which read, "CMI Investment Co., Richard P. Cavannaugh, President." This assured me he was from Ken White.

I asked, "Where's Ken?"

He replied, "Ken's in Hong Kong."

I said, "Well what's going on here? I've got money, receipts, notes, and I've got to get rid of this stuff. What's even more important, we've got another meeting in April."

He just said, "Let's go."

We went to his car and drove a short distance to a nearly deserted restaurant on a sidestreet. We sat down in a booth, and he leaned forward and said in quiet, measured tones, "Ken's in Hong Kong and I'm not authorized to debrief you. Just go home and wait. Ken will call you."

Our meeting ended, and I returned from Honolulu early.

I didn't suspect anything wrong at this point because I know from experience that a case officer occasionally has an impossible conflict and has to send an alternate to make a meeting with his agent. In this case, it resulted in a wasted trip to Honolulu.

I waited another week. When no call came from Ken, I dialed his hello phone again, gave my same message again, and waited. Nothing.

When I'd phoned in February, Ken himself called me back, but that turned out to be the last contact I ever had with him and the last time I ever heard his voice. The second time I tried to reach him was late March, and I tried again in mid-April. By then I'd missed the Vienna meeting window and was thoroughly discouraged.

I couldn't have gone to Vienna without the briefing and authorization to do so, nor could I go without a solution to the medical question. I really didn't give up hope of salvaging an important opportunity to capitalize on our hard-won espionage gains until I made one final try in mid-May but no one called back.

I couldn't believe the CIA would miss this opportunity to succeed in making an incursion of this magnitude without even contacting their agent. For the first time I had to face the real probability that something had gone wrong.

I wondered if Ken met with disaster or if there was a major policy decision at the top which had canceled the entire operation.

The actual truth could never really have occurred to me. The facts were that a business which fronted for the Agency's Honolulu operations was running wildly out of control, and everyone involved with it was disassociating and distancing himself from that company. It was like the rats were scurrying to abandon a sinking ship. I wasn't aware we were on such a ship, and nobody had even told me it had sprung a leak.

The biggest problem I would face was even more bizarre. The Agency—the CIA—was just then beginning to engineer one of the biggest cover-ups in its history, sweeping its Honolulu front-business under the rug.

The short-version name, "Bishop-Baldwin" is important at this point. It refers to a large Honolulu investment firm by the name of Bishop, Baldwin, Rewald, Dillingham and Wong that was about to collapse under charges of fraud and embezzlement. This CIA-front operation will figure prominently later.

Anyone experienced in intelligence operations knows that when an operation is canceled, the agent must disappear. He is never to try to contact his case officer. Disastrous things can happen, and have happened, to the "spy who came in out of the cold" on his own. So there I was, a former case officer myself, fully aware that I should make no further effort to contact Ken White, Danny Ishida, or for that matter, the CIA itself.

Unless I was sure there were extenuating circumstances, I was not to do so. Several other emergency conditions could merit that type of contact. If my life were in danger, I could, but it was not. If the nation's security hung in the balance, I might be justified, but I wasn't sure that it did.

If my good fortune at compromising Okunev had continued for the time and to the depth where the U.S. had their own "man in the Kremlin" how many lives could be saved? How much better could we defend against the Soviets? What unknown opportunities could our country take advantage of?

* * * * *

All during this time, I knew nothing of the CIA's problems in Honolulu nor of its attempt to cover them up. All I knew was that my country was about to lose one of the most significant intelligence opportunities it had ever had.

That was why on June 6th, 1983, I secretly flew to San Francisco, walked the short distance from the city airline terminal to the Federal Building, went to a pay phone in the lobby, and took the one step which would ultimately result in my arrest, my indictment by a grand jury as a spy, my imprisonment in Virginia, my trial for espionage, and the near loss of my freedom for a lifetime.

Because of the sensitivity of the operation, I chose to call the FBI and ask them to contact the CIA for me. I had to have "back door" access to the Agency, so I called an old FBI friend, Paul Shields, Chief of the Foreign Counterintelligence Squad in Oakland.

I said, "Paul, it's Craig. I need your help. I need to be in touch with the Agency. It doesn't involve the FBI. It doesn't involve your office, but it does involve contact overseas."

Paul was a trusted friend. He had been my bishop for the year-and-a-half we attended the Danville Ward of the Mormon Church, near Oakland. He knew exactly what I did for the Army, and as bishop, respected that mysterious privacy that isolated us from the rest of the church members. Further, he knew that "contact overseas" meant intelligence contact with governments hostile to the U.S.

I also knew he would routinely report our conversation to his superiors, but that didn't bother me because I had every reason to believe that both agencies were cooperating in monitoring my fully authorized activities. At worst, I would be criticized by Ken White or his boss for not simply waiting as I'd been told to.

Paul said, "Give me the number you're calling from and stand by the phone. I'll see what I can do."

I waited for a few minutes and Paul called back. "Okay," he said, "I reached them, and they'll call you."

He didn't give me their number, but after a few minutes more, the phone rang. A voice I didn't recognize asked, "Who are you?" I told him.

Then he asked, "What is this about?"

I said, "Look, you know what this is about. I want to talk—and not just over the phone." This was no time for phone games or for open-text codes.

The voice said, "Okay, I'm going to send somebody out to 'I.D.' you. Hold the line for another moment."

There was a pause, then a different voice said, "Where will I find you? What are you wearing?" I told him so he could identify me.

Then the first voice came again—but this time much closer to the mouthpiece, as if to threaten. "All right, Smith, you're into something you don't know anything about! I know what the situation is!" Then, menacingly, "Keep—your—(deleted)—mouth—shut!"

Voice number two probably had his coat on by now and was out the door to I.D. me, so voice number one, who obviously didn't need to identify me at all, repeated, "Smith, you keep your (vulgarity deleted) mouth shut! You don't say anything to anybody, especially to Shields and his people!"

I couldn't believe what I was hearing! At first it was professional-sounding conversation, and then suddenly I got a foulmouthed threat!

I said, "What are you talking about?"

"Just go home and keep your mouth shut! Go home and wait!"

I hung up the phone, waited, I.D.'d myself to the junior agent who showed up in twenty minutes, and then returned home to Salt Lake City.

On the plane home, the sound of the extreme agitation of the senior agent kept ringing in my ears, and the mystery was compounded by his emotional turmoil. A hundred questions suddenly shot through my head. I wondered who he was, how he was involved and whether or not I knew him. I even wondered if he had selected me for the Tokyo operation in the first place.

I wondered if he was Ken White's boss.

Why couldn't the CIA work with the FBI, and why couldn't my part of the operation go forward? Surely the operation was seen to be important.

If I had blundered into something, why was I such a threat to the voice on the phone? Since they had approached me, I couldn't understand why was the CIA treating me like this. The more I reflected, the more anxious I became.

I was furious. I was sick to think of the lost opportunities in Vienna and beyond, but I wasn't yet frightened. Whatever was happening, no harm could come to me. It was clear that they—the Agency—had a problem, but I didn't have a problem. The CIA wouldn't come after me, nor would the Soviets. I had total confidence in Paul Shields. After all, it was I who had gone to the FBI with a clear conscience and asked for help. I had certainly done nothing wrong, and it did not occur to me that I would ever become the object of an investigation.

By the time the plane landed in Salt Lake City on that June day in 1983, I was resigned to the fact that the operation was probably over. Even though the CIA voice had said, "Go home and wait," the tone of that voice told me it was probably history now.

I would forget Ken White and Danny Ishida. I would forget Viktor Okunev and the Soviets. I would forget Tokyo and Vienna.

I canceled a Timespan trip to Japan I had scheduled for that summer, to prevent any further contact with the KGB because I had no authority to do so. It was a tremendous disappointment, but I was resigned to it.

* * * * *

There were many unanswered questions—many things that I didn't understand until much later. However, we did uncover vast amounts of information months—even years—later, during our investigation which followed my arrest and release on bond.

First of all, the voice on the phone was that of Charles L. Richardson, alias Richard P. Cavannaugh. Richardson was a high-level CIA director of the Agency's San Francisco station, with authority over many operations throughout the Pacific. Most operations were fed through their clandestine cover in Honolulu: Bishop, Baldwin, Rewald, Dillingham and Wong, which was a major CIA proprietary.

The "authenticator" I was shown by Ken White and later by the male caucasian in Ala Moana Park, Danny II, was the ordinary business card of CMI Investment Co., a subsidiary of Bishop-Baldwin. As mentioned before, the name on the CMI card was "Richard P. Cavannaugh, President." Cavannaugh and Richardson were the same person, a case of multiple identities. This was legal, normal, and consistent with CIA and other intelligence practices.

It was an unfortunate coincidence that just as Ken White and I were ready to make our move into the KGB in Vienna, Bishop-Baldwin's house of cards began to tumble and, as a security measure, all operations were suddenly canceled.

The last thing Richardson/Cavannaugh needed was to have one of his terminated agents surface and raise a number of difficult questions, especially to the FBI, who at that moment was unaware of the breakdown in Honolulu.

Several extraordinary coincidences occurred as events unfolded, and coincidence number one was that Richardson/Cavannaugh was in the San Francisco CIA station office when Paul Shields' call came in. Since I have never been allowed access to the records which would inform me as to what happened, I constructed the most logical series of events. I used my knowledge of the agencies, people and their methods and fit these with the outcome. They fit well.

Paul probably said, "I have Craig Smith calling in, wanting to make contact with the Agency. Who should he talk to?"

When Richardson heard my name, it can be assumed he panicked, picked up the phone, attempted to contain me, and tried to keep me away from my friends at the FBI.

My call was routinely logged, and when we finally discovered the truth about Richardson and the unauthorized activities of the CIA, we put him on the witness stand. This later affected the outcome of my trial, but if anyone but Richardson had answered the phone that day, I might be in a federal prison right now!

* * * * *

The question has been asked of me a thousand times: Why did I try to contact my handlers in the CIA, thus breaking the very rules I learned to live by and enforce as a case officer?

I felt that I had at least equal—or possibly even more—experience than did Ken White, and I knew the potential value of our effort. Rather than let the operation fail, I easily justified re-contacting the CIA through the FBI.

Given the same situation, I'd probably do it again.

It's altogether possible—although sheer speculation on my part—that after he told me on the phone to "shut up," and "don't say anything to anybody—especially the FBI," Richardson/Cavannaugh could have picked up the phone immediately, dialed some one else in the FBI, and said, "We've just been contacted by a Craig Smith. We have reason to believe he's working for the Soviets. We suggest you get right on him, and pick him up."

10

The FBI Investigation

On a Saturday morning in July 1983, just a month after I'd talked on the phone with Paul Shields of the FBI, a knock came at the door of our home in North Salt Lake City.

My daughter answered the door and then came to me in the bedroom and said, "There are two men at the door to see you."

I went to the door and saw my old San Francisco FBI friend, Rick Smith, standing in the entry. I realized very quickly that this was no social call because both he and the agent with him flashed their FBI credentials when I opened the door.

"Do you know who I am?" he asked.

"Of course I do, Rick," I replied. "I know who you are."

"This is an official visit." He kept his credentials in front of my face. "Can we talk?"

"Sure. Here or outside?"

I didn't want to alarm my family or neighbors, so I said, "We could be alone at my office. There's no one there on Saturdays."

I dressed and drove the eight miles to the Timespan office with the FBI agents right behind me. I was apprehensive as this was sounding pretty serious, but I still had high hopes of reaching the right people in the CIA through the FBI.

THE FBI INVESTIGATION

By the time we'd settled into chairs at my office in downtown Salt Lake City, I realized that the problem was no longer that of just the CIA; it was rapidly becoming a problem for me, too.

Through my conversation with Paul Shields, the FBI knew I had made "contact overseas." It was necessary to fill in the details with a logical cover story, but I could not reveal that I was actually working for the CIA because I'd been told not to by the voice which I later learned was that of Richardson/Cavannaugh.

My only hope was to create a plausible story with glaring gaps that would cause them to check my story with the right people in the Agency. I reasoned that the CIA would then realize that one of their people was in trouble.

Rick started the conversation. He asked, "What's going on here?"

I answered, "Well, there's been contact in Japan with a KGB officer assigned to the commercial office of the Soviet Embassy."

"What kind of contact?" he asked me.

I told him I had met on several occasions with a KGB officer in Tokyo and had even persuaded him to give me a few thousand dollars to start a double-agent operation for my government.

I told Rick repeatedly that my story was a CIA matter, and that if he and his people would check with the Agency, they'd get the rest of the story. Over and over I would leave blank spaces or missing details out of my story, hoping they'd go to the CIA for the remaining pieces and thus let the right people know about the trouble I was getting into.

Why didn't I just blow the whistle, call time out, and tell them everything? As it turned out, it might have been wiser to have done so, because I later discovered I wasn't protecting anyone's life or the CIA itself or its other operations. All these possibilities had melted when Bishop-Baldwin started to crumble in Honolulu. The reason I didn't tell them about CIA involvement is that I was trained from my early years to follow orders, and my orders were clear, "Keep your mouth shut . . . about CIA details, . . . especially to the FBI!"

My intelligence training told me that I could endanger the lives of other agents or at the least destroy other operations if I crossed taht line and revealed the CIA details of my case.

Much later, after five weeks in solitary confinement, it became clear to me that the only thing I was protecting was Richardson/Cavannaugh's skin, and I was trading my freedom for his.

There are several possibilities as to why my desperate signals didn't bring help. Since I have never had the courtesy of an explanation, I am left with the necessity of reasoning their behavior for myself.

First of all, if the FBI ever did talk to the CIA, it's least likely, but possible, that the right people never got the message. It's more likely that they did get the message, but the larger objective(s) had to take priority to protect operational identities and activities. However, it's most likely that they not only got my message, they needed me put away to avoid any more disclosures about what was happening in Honolulu—or any other subsequent embarrassments—than were absolutely necessary.

It is even possible that the FBI never did check my story with the CIA or waited too long to do so, and my situation had deteriorated beyond salvage. There is a certain mind-set in the make-up of investigating agents that allows them to hear just those answers that bring them closer to their investigative goals. The clues, hints, and gaps that I repeatedly tried to get through to them may never have registered because these signals didn't help them develop their case against me.

On the second day of the FBI's investigation. I gave Rick one scenario that was so off-the-wall that he said, "Wait a minute! That doesn't even make sense."

I replied, "That's right, Rick, it doesn't, but if you'll check with the CIA, it will."

I doubt that Rick ever even heard my answer because it would have complicated his report. This was the same Rick Smith with whom I had worked on joint projects when I was in charge of the

San Francisco office of Special Operations on the seventh floor of the Federal Building. He was on the eighth.

At the trial Rick had to testify against me. It must have been difficult, but he had his marching orders and he obeyed them. Not that it was difficult for FBI people to incriminate me when they testified under oath at my trial. Heaven knows my twisted cover story was only partially true and was a fabricated concealment of any number of missing facts.

Plainly, I withheld information from the FBI to protect the CIA, its operations, its agents, and even those who had acted well beyond their authority.

I was interviewed by the FBI twelve to fifteen times during the eight months prior to my arrest, by various people in various places, in Salt Lake City, Seattle and Washington D.C. During every interview, I maintained my silence about my actual role with the CIA. I would send messages, drop hints, and try every way possible to communicate information to them that would lead them back to the CIA and somehow make the connection that would exonerate me.

At this point, and right up until I was released on bond after five weeks in a Virginia jail, I really believed that whatever it was that had gone wrong would be resolved eventually. When that day came, somebody would be able to come in and say, "Okay, call off the dogs. He's one of ours." I was totally convinced that my loyalty to the Agency would be recognized and that loyalty would be returned.

That loyalty never has been, and probably never will be, returned. In short, the CIA never came forward, publicly or secretly. I knew better than to try to contact them again. When they tell you to "go home and wait" they don't give you any options.

I lost count of how many polygraph tests the FBI gave me. At first, every time I'd agree to another "poly," the operator would say when he was finished, "There's nothing wrong here. He's telling the truth."

Unfortunately, these tests are inadmissible in court. I say unfortunately because the fact that I passed so many polygraphs would have influenced a jury positively. It's interesting to note, as a matter of record, that in pretrial hearings, the government wanted to be allowed to say that "We gave the defendant polygraph exams, but we won't reveal the results."

This would have influenced the jury negatively. Fortunately, the judge saw through this and disallowed any mention of polygraphs.

The fact is, I gave them the truth, but not the whole story. I couldn't. As I'd said again and again to Rick Smith, "This isn't all—there's more to it than this, but I can't tell you any more. You'll have to bring in the CIA." They never did.

Instead, on one occasion they brought my former boss, Noel Jones, the fellow who said I'd never work for the government again, out from Maryland. He pleaded with me to tell "the rest of the story."

I said, "I can't do it, but I'll tell you right now that I did not give the Soviets any unauthorized information."

The key clue was that I did not say "classified" information. I said "unauthorized." If information is not "unauthorized," it could only have been "authorized." By whom was is authorized? They would never ask me.

Having replied to Jones with this declaration, I was asked, "Would you take a polygraph on that?"

I replied, "Sure, as long as you use the word 'unauthorized.' "

I took another poly, and again the examiner said, "There's no problem here." Then, ironically, he added, "I'm convinced he hasn't given away any unauthorized information."

Noel Jones then shook my hand and said, "Congratulations! I knew you wouldn't let us down!" He left on good terms, very different from the last time we had parted company.

Later, during my trial, Jones was asked if I'd been authorized to give information about double-agent operations, and he replied, "I didn't authorize it."

Again everyone missed the point. It wasn't his job in my case to authorize it. It was up to the CIA, which has an authority superior to that of all other government intelligence agencies, to authorize anything.

It was sloppy investigative work on the part of the FBI. It was also in part the "prosecutorial" mind-set I spoke of earlier. Mostly it was the scent of blood—"We've got a bust coming here, so don't confuse the issue with anything that doesn't fit."

In December of 1983, Rick Smith brought Ron Hilly, the same poly examiner I'd been seeing regularly, to the Excelsior Hotel in Provo, Utah, since we were then living in nearby Orem. Once again I agreed to take a lie-detector test. I was getting very annoyed at the failure of the government to get the matter resolved.

After the test Rick said to me, "As far as I'm concerned this is over because there isn't anything here. We have no evidence that you've done anything wrong, other than what you've said you've done. You said you've given the Soviets no unauthorized information, and you've established that on polygraph. So as far as I'm concerned the investigation is over."

With this, I thought it was finished. I was relieved that the ordeal was finally over. I moved my family to Seattle in February of 1984 and started to develop my new career as an international marketing consultant.

Three days after my arrival I got a call from Rick Smith. "Craig, it's not over yet. We need to talk to you one more time. Would you be willing to meet two other people from the Bureau in Seattle?"

This time I started getting angry and said, "Look, Rick, we've been through it time and time again. I've passed the polys. You know that there isn't anything I'm going to tell you until you agree to bring the Agency into this."

Basically, I told him I didn't want to do it. In every single interview, I'd told Rick that I couldn't tell them any more until they brought the CIA into the picture. I said, "Rick, you'd be wasting your time and mine. I'm not going to tell you anything I haven't already told you."

He said, "Look. Just do this for me. Please do it."

"Okay, I'll do it."

I entered the lobby of the Pacific Plaza Hotel in downtown Seattle and met two more FBI agents, Mike Waguespack and Bill Schmitz. They escorted me to an FBI car and drove me to their Seattle headquarters in the Federal Building.

The Federal Building, Seattle, Washington. Photo by Larry Dion courtesy of Seattle Times.

Waguespack did most of the talking. "We appreciate your coming. We'd like to go through this one more time."

I said, "Look. We've been through this enough, so here are the rules. I haven't disclosed any unauthorized information. I have had contact with the Soviets. I know that the Soviet I spoke to is an intelligence officer. I know that there were conversations you may be concerned about, but I've told you that I haven't given anything that was unauthorized, and I've passed polygraph examinations to establish that. I'm not going to say any more than that, other than the fact that this is not an FBI matter. It's a CIA matter. Do you get the message? Bring in someone from the CIA and I'll talk!"

They still wouldn't do it. They said, "Well, we'd like you to take another polygraph."

I demurred again, for two reasons. First, as I had said so many times already, there was nothing new to discuss. Second, every succeeding time a polygraph examiner goes over the same questions, the more manipulative it can become. The examinee can finally be made to appear to be lying because it's no longer spontaneous. The second time around, you're subconsciously anticipating the same questions, and this somehow triggers physiological responses similar to those caused by the act of lying. Then each succeeding time, as you become more familiar with the wording of the questions, this anticipation response grows stronger, so the chances to manipulate you into self-incrimination increase.

I finally gave in, and they took me into a private room and introduced me to a new polygraph examiner—not Ron Hilly this time. As we proceeded, it was clear by the nature of his questions that the new examiner was out to create a situation that could be interpreted as a lie. About halfway through I stopped the exam and began removing the apparatus.

I went back into the original conference room and said to Waguespack, "I'm not going any further with this exam."

He asked, "Why not?"

"Because this new examiner is trying to manipulate the results of the test, that's why."

When the examiner was asking me about various operations, including the six which I'd been directed by the CIA to give to Okunev, he refused to play by the rules. He asked if I'd given any information at all about a dozen or so operations. This included "Lancer Flag," "Landscape Breeze," "Canary Dance," "Hole Punch," "Lariat Toss," and "Royal Miter," which were the names of the six operations actually authorized by the Agency. All six were dead issues by then, some having been terminated many years before. I wasn't going to let him manipulate me into appearing to lie.

Mike Waguespack then singled out one of the operations—I'm still not at liberty to disclose which one—and told me the FBI was concerned because "something funny was going on" with the agent involved.

The red flag went up because this was the first time any mention was made of current happenings even though I immediately had to suspect that Waguespack was bluffing or lying to trap me into a confession of some kind. If this were true, and if I were guilty of treason, he had absolutely no business telling this information to a Soviet spy.

I simply denied knowing anything about such a development, and they released me to return home.

It was early afternoon as I drove across the Lake Washington bridge to my parents' home in Bellevue, and as I drove, I thought, what if Waguespack could possibly be telling me the truth. Then it could mean that even though the operation was terminated long ago, either the Soviets were testing me by trying to recontact this agent, or the FBI was testing both the Soviets and me by reactivating him.

There could be two consequences of each of these possible scenarios.

In the first, if the Soviets were testing me by trying to recontact someone they now knew was a double agent, and if I remained silent and thus the agent wasn't warned, he could walk into a Soviet trap and be killed. However, if I disobeyed CIA orders and revealed the details of the CIA's involvement—to make sure the agent was warned—the Soviets would realize I was a double agent and come after me.

On the other hand, if FBI people were testing both the Soviets and me by reactivating this agent (by telling him it was safe to recontact the Soviets) my silence would surely get him killed. If I told the whole CIA story to the FBI in order to warn the agent, I could be disavowed by the CIA, convicted of espionage, and spend the rest of my life in prison.

In short, if Waguespack was telling the truth, a life—mine or the agent's—was at risk. If he was not, I could be prosecuted as a confessed spy. Thus, if Waguespack was truthful—and I had to allow for that possibility—either the FBI was using me to test the Soviets, or the Soviets were using me to test American intelligence. Either way, I found myself in a desperate, no-win situation!

By the time I pulled my car into the driveway, I was really concerned. I wasn't scared, but I was deeply concerned. Here was the FBI not talking to the CIA, the CIA not talking to the FBI, and nobody was listening to me. With two agents' lives at stake—mine and another's—I had a decision to make, and it was a tough one.

There were no national security secrets involved. This agent no longer had access to any classified information and yet his life was on the line. And so was mine. I walked in the door of my father's home in Bellevue, found Susan, and took her out on the patio where we would be alone.

I said, "Sue, I'm involved in something here, and I think you know that. I still can't tell you what it is, but I've got to make a decision, and it's the hardest decision I've ever had to make in my life. There's a very real possibility that a man's life is at stake, and I don't know what to do. If I do what I've been told to do, somebody might get hurt. Somebody could even die. If I do what I've been told not to do, it's...."

My voice broke. I paused, then continued. "It's very possible the government will come after me because I'm going to have to violate a secrecy agreement that I've made. If I do that, they're going to be very unhappy with me. I don't know what to do."

We went down to the basement bedroom where we were staying, and knelt beside the bed. We prayed. We prayed for guidance in making this decision. I said, "Lord, I've got to know what I should do!"

I got up, went over to the phone—it was still mid-afternoon—and called Mike Waguespack. I said, "Mike, we need to talk."

He said, "Can you come back this afternoon?"

I said, "No, I've got to sort a few things out, but I'll be in tomorrow. There are some things I think we need to talk about."

I went back in the next day.

I said, "It's important for you to know that this certain agent has been discussed."

I still remained true to my CIA orders. I didn't tell them it was the CIA who authorized me to, but I did say, "It had been authorized."

I also said, "There was no breach of security, but I was authorized to give the Soviets information about 'Lancer Flag,' 'Landscape Breeze,' 'Canary Dance,' 'Hole Punch,' 'Lariat Toss,' and 'Royal Miter.'"

I didn't say who authorized it. That was the balancing act. Mike didn't ask me, either. That was the mystery.

Then I told Mike, "What you need to do is to go back to your people in Washington D.C. and have them get in touch with the people at Langley (the CIA's headquarters in Virginia), and when you have done that, you give me a call."

Then I went home. On the phone a day or two later, we agreed that the best thing to do was to fly me to FBI headquarters in Washington D.C., meet with Bill Schmitz and Mike Waguespack and hash out the details close to where the CIA is headquartered. It appeared that finally we might be getting nearer to bridging the gap.

They agreed, bought my ticket to Washington, and arranged for a hotel room just outside of Washington D.C.

* * * * *

At FBI headquarters in Washington, the same polygraph examiner was there—the one who tried to manipulate me in Seattle—and they wanted to do another polygraph. I was apprehensive, but agreed to another poly, mostly because I had a new story to tell now.

You see, I'd spent eight months building cover stories to obey the CIA order to keep quiet, and now I thought I had to tell them every

The J. Edgar Hoover Building, headquarters of the Federal Bureau of Investigation in Washington, D.C. Photo by Lisa C. Ure.

thing in order to save an agent's life. It was soon obvious however, that all the examiner wanted to do was to prove I was lying, so he got more and more manipulative.

After three days of this, I was getting increasingly nervous about the poly results for the reasons discussed before. I felt I was getting to the point emotionally where I was incapable of passing a poly. Eventually the results would begin to read "inconclusive" again and again, which tends to incriminate. That's why I finally told them I wouldn't take any more polygraphs. I told them I was going home, and that they should sort this all out and call me if they needed more information.

* * * * *

During my stay in Virginia, the surveillance was unbelievable. Six or eight agents were on my tail every minute. I could see them everywhere. Behind power poles, around corners—it was almost ludicrous. It must have been an exercise for new trainees. I thought I should send them a bill for training their people. The surveillance continued in Seattle.

As my wife and I headed for the Bridge and Bellevue, it was so blatant that I decided to show it to Susan before she discovered it on her own.

I said, "Susan, we're being followed by the FBI, and we're probably going to be followed until we get this resolved."

I said, "See the silver Firebird behind us?" I pointed out the car following us.

She said, "No, he's not following us!"

"You watch!"

I pulled a couple of quick maneuvers, and it took only two or three minutes to convince her that he was following us. Then I pointed out two other cars.

From that time on, surveillance became obtrusive—even dangerous. If I had stopped suddenly, there would have been a four-car pile-up. They would park two or three cars in front of my parents' home, and even the neighbors became alarmed.

I got angry. This was nonsense.

I thought, I'm not trying to run away; I'm not trying to hide anything; I've not done anything wrong; I've cooperated. What is all this?

One day, using some very basic countersurveillance techniques, I slipped out of the net they had established around my father's house. I had Susan drive me around the block and then go back into the driveway. I slid down low and she drove out again. She appeared to be alone, so they stayed at the house, thinking I'd gone back inside.

We drove to the FBI office in Seattle, where I walked in and said, "I want to talk to the supervisor or whoever's in charge of surveillance on Smith!"

They said, "What's this all about?"

"Well, I'm Smith, and your people are still sitting around my father's house!"

The agent there got on the phone—obviously talking to the surveillance chief—and said, "Smith's sitting in my office."

I told them, "Look, I don't appreciate all this intimidating presence around my home, and I'm not going to tolerate it. I want you to get Waguespack on the phone right now and this is what I want you to tell him. Tell him I'm not going to put up with it, that I can slip it anytime I want, and I'll make life very miserable for you guys. On the other hand, I don't want to have to be in that mode either. I want to resolve this thing once and for all. You tell Waguespack. . . ."

The man at the desk interrupted. "You tell Mr. Waguespack. He's on the line now."

I took the phone and said, "Mike, I'm going to be back there tomorrow afternoon, and I'm paying my own way. I'm not leaving Washington until we get this resolved. If you guys are going to come after me, if you insist on making life miserable for me and my parents and their neighborhood, then you might as well go ahead and arrest me now if you're going to arrest me ever, because obviously that's the direction you're taking!

"I'll be there tomorrow afternoon. Get me a motel room at the government rate, and I'll pay for that, too. I'm not going to impose any more of your intimidation on my family, so plan on my arrival tomorrow. Only don't expect to talk to me until the afternoon following because I have other business in the morning."

I hung up the phone, went back home and called a close friend in Maryland, the psychiatrist, Dr. Joseph Smith. We'd known each other since we'd lived in Pacific Grove while I was attending language school. I asked him if he'd let me spend the morning in his office, exploring the possible use of truth serum, hypnosis, and polygraphs to prove my innocence.

* * * * *

When I arrived at Dulles Airport the surveillance was heavier than ever, but I spent the next morning with Joe and got the information I needed.

Joe was a brilliant man and a trusted friend. A medical doctor and a psychiatrist, he also had a law degree. I wanted to know both the safety and fairness of truth serum, hypnosis, and polygraphs because I had a plan to force the FBI's hand.

It was no surprise that polygraphs were the least reliable and most manipulative, but I was interested in his comments on the other two.

Joe said, "Craig, truth serum is the most reliable, and is relatively safe medically if you have nothing to hide. If you're hiding anything at all, they can dig it out with truth serum."

He continued, "Hypnosis is the next most reliable, but it can also be used to reach hidden information."

I asked, "Joe, if the FBI is willing to administer one or more of these to allow me to prove once and for all that I'm telling the truth, would you be willing to be present to be sure they don't manipulate me or endanger me physically? He agreed, and I returned to my motel room to meet Mike Waguespack.

"Mike," I said, "I've spent the morning with Dr. Joseph Smith."

I gave him Joe's credentials, and told him what we'd been talking about.

I said, "Here's the plan. I'm prepared to undergo—one at a time—truth serum, hypnosis, and/or more polygraphs—whatever it takes to establish what the whole truth is. Remember, as I've said already, I haven't told you the whole story yet. I can't tell you the whole story. It's not that I'm trying to hide anything; I've been told not to."

Once more they wouldn't ask, "By whom?"

"I'll tell you the whole truth. I'll tell you everything. You can inject, probe, put me under, put needles in my arm, anything you want to do. These are the conditions. Number one, Dr. Smith must be present, so that he can be sure you don't manipulate me while I'm under. Number two is that a representative of the CIA must be present." This was to assure that the CIA could not ignore my story and would be forced to get at the truth.

I don't know if it was a smart thing to do, but I desperately needed to call the FBI's bluff and get to the real truth.

I told Mike, "I'll sign a release absolving you of any medical liability. I'll sign a waiver allowing anything I say to be used against me in court. You can bring in a doctor from the CIA or anyone else you want to bring in. You can ask any question you want to as long as it's not manipulative. I'm going to put the whole truth on the table. I'll sign anything to absolve you of any responsibility and give you every opportunity to incriminate me. You can have it all your way."

He said, "Okay, we'll take your proposal back to headquarters and talk about it."

I waited in the hotel room until Waguespack called, saying he'd be back in about an hour or so.

When he returned, he said, "We ran your proposal by the Bureau, but they won't accept it."

It was what I was afraid to hear, but somehow I expected it. I looked squarely at Mike Waguespack and said, "Mike, it occurs to me, and it probably ought to occur to you, that it doesn't really matter whether I tell you the truth or not, does it? Because, even if I tell you the truth, you're coming after me. Isn't that right?"

Mike couldn't look me in the eye. He stood at the foot of the motel bed, put his head down a bit and nervously shuffled his feet a little.

I challenged him. "Mike, that's true, isn't it?"

And without even looking up, he just said, "Well, it's not the way I'd have wanted it...." More foot movement. "But I guess that's the truth."

I said, "That's all I need to know."

We tried to introduce this conversation at my trial, but the government objected. It could not be allowed because of a technicality—the word "polygraph" was in there.

It seemed unfair to me. We could have put Waguespack on the stand, and he would have had to admit this exchange took place.

Meanwhile I said, "Well, if you're going to come after me regardless of where the truth lies, let's get on with it. Get on the phone to your supervisor and tell him I'm turning myself in. Arrest me—here—now!" I put my hands out for the handcuffs.

Mike picked up the phone and dialed his boss, and then afterwards, turned back to me and said, "No, we want you to go home."

"Well then, I want to speak to an attorney. You've read me my rights, and I'm entitled to a lawyer."

Mike said, "But we haven't charged you with anything. You're not entitled to a lawyer until charges have been filed."

The conversation was going nowhere, so I asked to be taken to the airport, and I boarded a plane for the return trip to Seattle.

It was only after my release from jail that I learned why they were not willing to arrest me at that time. It was because they had not yet completed planning a well-organized press campaign designed to discredit me.

We know this because of internal memos we subpoenaed from the FBI. Among them was one which clearly shows that the arrest date was delayed to allow the press to be given advance notice.

In addition, my eventual arrest date "just happened" to fall on the day that hearings were held on capitol hill for more counter-espionage funds for the FBI's budget. One of my attorneys still believes the huge surveillance numbers were for the purpose of piling up man-hours for budget statistics.

I went home again and waited, this time for fourteen days.

11

My Arrest & Imprisonment

It was hard to concentrate on getting work to bring in a little income. I had just taken a temporary position writing resumes and had been back in Seattle again only two weeks when the phone rang. Again it was the FBI asking me to come back to Washington once more "to talk to us one more time."

"We'll buy your ticket and have an agent come out and pick you up and take you to the airport. Let's see if we can't get this thing settled. Would you be willing to come out one more time?"

I answered, "I'll come out every day, if we can just get this thing resolved."

An agent picked me up early on the morning of April 4th, 1984, and I recognized him as one of those who had been part of the Seattle surveillance.

Riding to the airport in an FBI car was a stressful experience because I didn't know whether I'd be arrested on my arrival in D.C. or not. Looking back, my attorneys and I are convinced now that had I refused to go, this agent had orders to arrest me on the spot. In fact, in pretrial hearings, we attempted to get my trial moved to Seattle, based on the presumption that I was actually arrested in Bellevue.

When I arrived at Dulles Airport, I was immediately met by Mike Waguespack and another agent and placed under arrest.

They put on the handcuffs and led me to their car. They followed the standard procedure with Mike removing his weapon out of his shoulder-holster and placing it on the floor of the front seat, away from the grasp of a prisoner who rode with him in the back.

While I didn't actually expect it, I wasn't terribly surprised. I even tried to be pleasant about it. The agents were both apologetic, they seemed even somewhat intimidated, and it was plain to see their hearts were not in this at all. They seemed to be agonizing over having to do it to me, and they scarcely looked at me. I attempted to ease some of the tension by mentioning a basketball game the previous night, but got no response.

Finally, Mike said, "Look. Let's not make this any more difficult than it has to be."

The FBI field office in Alexandria, Virginia. Photo by Lisa C. Ure.

On the way to the Alexandria, Virginia, field office of the FBI, news of my arrest came over the car radio. The press had been awarded its scoop, obviously even before the arrest had taken place. Within hours, video footage of the arrest was being flashed across the country in network newsbreaks.

After fingerprinting and other details were taken care of at the FBI office, we didn't get back in the car to drive the two blocks down to the Fairfax County courthouse for my arraignment. I was forced to walk between two agents—in handcuffs—to provide the "photo opportunities" promised to the assembled press.

The newspapers and magazines published my picture with a "hangdog" look on my face. Those photographers are smart. They wait for you at the next curb, and the moment a prisoner in handcuffs looks down to check his footing, they snap another "guilty" photo.

The Fairfax County Courthouse in Alexandria, Virginia. Photo by Lisa C. Ure.

It was well after six o'clock in the evening when we arrived at the courthouse, but the lights burned brightly and the reception had been well planned. The press waited anxiously, and the questions came from every direction.

The magistrate was ready to arraign me the moment we arrived. Reporters, photographers, and TV crews were everywhere, but only sketch-artists were allowed in the actual courtroom.

The magistrate read the charges filed by the Justice Department: two counts of espionage, two counts of passing secrets to the Soviets, and one count of conspiracy. These charges related only to one of the six operations the CIA had authorized me to pass. The other five were never mentioned.

I was asked how I would plead, and I answered, "Not guilty."

Then the question, "Are you represented by counsel?"

I had no choice. I had to ask for a court-appointed attorney. I had neither time to select a lawyer, nor did I have the funds to pay for private counsel.

For these reasons, I claimed indigency. This triggered an annoying series of questions to verify my need for a court-appointed attorney.

"What is your income? Does your wife work, and where? Whose home are you and your family living in? What is your telephone number? Name your children, their ages, and where do they attend school."

It seemed that this was more for the benefit of the press than for any legal requirement. The media could now send reporters to harass and attempt interviews with my parents, wife, and children. Fortunately, the schools in Bellevue protected my children's privacy, and they were never subjected to this humiliation.

Before being led out of the magistrate's courtroom, the U.S. marshals put me in chains at my waist which led to irons around my wrists and ankles. I asked if they expected me to walk the two blocks back to the FBI office, and the marshals said no, a sedan was waiting close to the rear entrance.

MY ARREST & IMPRISONMENT

The walkway to the Fairfax County Courthouse in Alexandria, Virginia. Photo by Lisa C. Ure.

A marshal's car is always pulled up as close as possible to an exit to prevent attacks, escapes, or suicide attempts, but when we reached the door, I could see the car parked at the far side of the underground parking lot, with an array of reporters, T.V. crews, and photographers waiting anxiously to record the FBI's "victory" over espionage.

If this weren't bad enough, the marshals on each arm obviously had been told to walk slowly for the cameras. I tried to drag them faster through the media, but was forced to endure the ultimate humiliation of being photographed like some kind of chained animal being led to its punishment. I wondered if this was really still my country, the U.S. of A.

I remember wondering if the networks would include the Justice Department when they rolled the credits at the end of each news program because they couldn't have had more help with the staging.

I was taken to the Fairfax County jail where I was again fingerprinted, then booked, photographed, and had my belongings, my belt and my shoelaces taken from me.

I was placed in a holding cell, six by eight feet, with a concrete bench, for thirty hours. No mattress, no blanket, no pillow—nothing. Bright, glaring fluorescent lights were left on without relief. It was freezing cold. I had nothing but a blazer over a sweater which I alternately used for a pillow, then a blanket.

At that point, my primary concern was for Susan and the children. How would they handle the avalanche of news reports?

In the numbness of exhaustion, there was a strange sense of surrealism. This wasn't happening! It felt like I was drifting in and out of my body. I'd wake up and wonder where I was.

I finally woke up to a couple of slices of bread and a small bowl of cereal for breakfast, but I was almost too exhausted to eat. I looked at the cell across the hall and a gnome-like character with a huge nose and a frightfully hairy face and head stared back at me. He looked as if he were strung out and waiting till he was straight enough to be processed. His appearance was so unreal it seemed like some sort of comic strip fantasy.

The fear and agonizing over the feelings of my wife and children brought me back to reality again and again. Finally on the afternoon following my evening arraignment, I was allowed my first phone call. I called Susan.

She was terrified and confused, having learned of the arrest at work the day before. She and my parents had had no word from me for twenty-four hours. I told her that I was all right and not to worry about me, that everything was going to turn out okay, and we'd be together again soon.

MY ARREST & IMPRISONMENT

To fully understand what Susan and I were going through, it is essential to know of the last conversation I had with her and my parents the night before flying to my arrest in Virginia.

We talked that night about a phone call I'd received a few days earlier from my former secretary in Salt Lake City, Mavis Nelson. Mavis had told me that a Pete Chase from the FBI had been in to talk to her, and in the course of their conversation, he had inadvertently let her know that the FBI knew that I'd been working for the CIA. At first it hadn't sunk in. Then it hit me. This FBI agent, Pete Chase, had made a major mistake, but it was clearly in my favor. The last thing either the FBI or the CIA wanted me to know is that they had been talking. His inadvertently telling her this was the next thing to a miracle, and it became a significant issue at the trial.

I had called Mavis back immediately that day and said, "Mavis, listen carefully. I want you to sit down and make an accurate, stenographic transcript of your conversation with Chase. It might be the most important piece of evidence I'll have. Mail me a copy, and put a copy in a safe deposit box." She had done so, and it had arrived before I left Bellevue.

The night before I left I had called my parents and Susan together and told them for the first time that for over thirty months I'd been working for the CIA, and that we'd finally gotten the first piece of evidence to prove that the FBI was aware of my CIA contacts. I had shown them Mavis's letter and said, "No matter what happens, even if they arrest me, you have to trust me."

I went on, "I can't tell you all of the details, and I don't know if I'll ever be able to tell you everything, but I'm telling you this right now. I've not done anything wrong, and if I'm accused of anything, it will be a false accusation.

"If I do find that I've done something I didn't know was illegal, I'll tell you, but right now I'm positive that I haven't done anything wrong. I'm innocent and I'm certain that in a court of law I'll be able to prove this. I hope we won't have to go through that, but I think you'd better be prepared because this could happen."

Then, as a united family, my parents and Susan and I had knelt down together and prayed that the situation could be resolved without having to go through the agony of a court case against me. However, if we had to go to court, this letter that Mavis had mailed and had put in a safe deposit box would be one of the bricks that would eventually strengthen my case and vindicate me.

It had been very painful, not only sitting down and telling my wife and parents all this, but telling them that I might even be arrested and jailed.

My inner fears were even more painful during the last fourteen days of my freedom because I then knew that the FBI, even after talking to the CIA, was unwilling to acknowledge the truth. I didn't know why at the time because I was still unaware of the Agency's difficulties in Honolulu.

I had no idea why they were coming after me rather than coming after the truth. My most private fear was that rather than arrest me, a decision might be reached to create an "accident"—a more final solution. Still, I was hopeful that the CIA would eventually solve its problem—whatever it was—and return me to my family and to a normal life.

For all of these reasons, in our family prayer I had turned the problem over to the Lord, and I knew that He would keep my family safe. I had faith that He would touch the hearts of the good people in our government, and that He could, if necessary, cause a miracle to happen if one of His children were in trouble.

Besides, my faith in my government was still unshaken, and I felt I'd be exonerated anyway. I did, however, recognize the importance of the Lord's hand in restoring our family unit once again.

During my first phone call from jail, I reassured Susan that I was physically all right and told her to remember our discussion two days earlier about the letter from Mavis Nelson. No matter what happened, I was innocent and the truth would eventually be known. I knew this call was being monitored, but it didn't matter. The important thing was to help my family keep their faith in me.

In the Fairfax County jail there are four divisions, and I'd been held in the first section, or holding cell, for thirty hours, then transferred to the classification section for three days. There they put me in a cell which openly joined five others by day but was locked by night. I was given prison clothing in exchange for my own, showered, deloused and otherwise dehumanized, and then given a complete physical examination.

I was interviewed at length about my age, my civilian status, and my alleged crime in order to classify me for assignment to a permanent cell. I would be in either of the two other sections: the general population or administrative segregation.

Life in classification went on for three days. I managed to talk to Susan each day, and the numbness I spoke of gradually began to wear off.

Across the hall there was a black inmate with whom I would speak occasionally. He would read his Bible, and we'd sit across a table we shared by daytime, and sometimes we'd talk. I greatly appreciated his quiet friendship, especially on the third day in classification, when the reality of my separation from my family really hit me.

I called Susan that day and began the conversation pretty much in control. Susan was telling me that one of the women in our church congregation had offered to take Ian into her preschool, free, to help pull us through.

When Susan said Ian's name, I broke down emotionally. Suddenly it hit me—more deeply than ever before—that I might never see my son again, at least not in the setting that I'd known before.

I broke down on the phone and wept openly. The picture of someone else caring for my son was too much. Susan was crying too, but I finally managed to gain control again and finished the conversation.

The tall, black inmate had been standing in the doorway of his cell, watching me. When I came back to the block—we were the only two in that area—he walked over to me, handed me his Bible, put his hand on my shoulder, and said, "The Man will take care of them."

It was a nice feeling to know, if only for a moment, that somebody could touch me—that somebody cared.

From that moment on, as I transferred on to administrative segregation, the loneliness grew, and the sense of isolation and helplessness was devastating.

The first phone call from my court-appointed attorney, William B. Cummings, came on my first day in classification. Bill was a former U.S. Attorney. He told me later that he felt they had selected him because he had just left the Justice Department for private practice, and his government security clearance would be the easiest to renew. This was important because classified government documents would be involved in my defense.

We did not meet until I had been assigned out of classification the next day, but he told me he was concerned about my being moved to the general population. In these cellblocks there were television sets on every floor and my arrest was known to every inmate, including an assortment of veterans of various wars, both real and imagined.

The possibility of constant physical danger was very real in the general population. We didn't need some Rambo carrying out his own arbitrary justice. So Cummings asked for—and got—my assignment to administrative segregation.

I was assigned to my own cell in one of the blocks there. It was terrible to be in a kind of solitary confinement, but it was much safer. The noise was deafening; radios blared rock music from different stations all at once. Voices yelled obscenities. Metal banged on metal. Heavy steel doors opened and slammed shut twenty-four hours a day.

In segregation, inmates couldn't see or reach anyone, so they yelled and shouted through the cinderblock walls to each other—or to anyone—to keep from going crazy. The profanity was the worst I had ever been exposed to. Finally I bought my own transistor radio from the prison commissary and played nothing but classical music. I was not popular.

My memories of isolation in my segregated cell in the Fairfax County jail were horrible, but I kept reminding myself that I wasn't in the open battlefield of the population, that I wasn't in a Soviet cell in Lubjanka, that I could talk to Susan every day, and that my family was safe.

I fully believed that one day soon a knock would come at the door, and the guard's voice would say, "These guys down the hall want to see you." I'd be taken down to the visitors' room where some CIA people would say, "We're very sorry for what has happened. . . ." It would be all over. I really believed that.

Susan's father, Mitchell Woods, was among the first of many family members to visit me. He cut short a business trip in the area, and brought me a copy of a book titled *Jesus the Christ*.

In spite of the awful food, the obnoxious guards, and the constant profanity, Fairfax began to feel like a weird sort of home—and even took on a kind of warped peace that's hard to describe.

I spent countless hours reading my scriptures, much time in meditation, and more time on my knees in prayer than at any time in my life.

I prayed for my family and friends to trust me and wait for the truth to surface. I also prayed for Susan and the children to endure this horrible separation, for the good people in government to have their hearts softened and hear the truth, for my attorneys to make good decisions and for the courage to endure to the end. Finally, I asked for help in continuing to walk that tightrope between the truth and my duty to national security.

Every single one of these prayers was answered, and miracles were sent from Heaven in form and number that were beyond comprehension.

* * * * *

I met with my two attorneys soon after my assignment to segregation. Since they had to go into court soon and tell the judge something of the basis for my not guilty plea, they kept asking me for the full story and again I had to say, "There's more to this than I can tell you."

Once more I was forced to choose. I could hold back and lose my case for lack of evidence in my own defense, or I could tell them everything and betray my patriotic duty to my country to maintain secrecy. It even occurred to me that I could be released, have the charges dropped, and then have the government charge me with breach of my security agreement.

For this reason my two attorneys, Bill Cummings and Brent Carruth, a second attorney we'd retained from California, would meet with me in the visitors' area and ask me questions I simply wouldn't answer. They'd say, "How can we help you if you won't give us the whole story?"

In my early days in jail I'd reply, "I can't. The government apparently has a problem which will soon be resolved, and then they'll drop the charges and release me anyway."

It sounded so absurd to them that the attorneys decided to start working on a defense strategy of "diminished capacity," claiming that the intense stress of thirteen years of counterintelligence work had impaired my ability to discern right from wrong. I would have been led by my own foggy thinking into trying to start a double-agent operation on my own. It was the kind of defense that bordered on "temporary insanity." I wanted no part of it and told them so.

They told me they stood a chance of getting me off with a light sentence—maybe just a year or a few years in a psychiatric hospital.

However, I'd done nothing wrong, and I knew I hadn't. Furthermore, I knew exactly what I was doing. So as the days and weeks wore on, I steadfastly refused to consider such a plea.

On the other hand, the "rescue" by the CIA wasn't happening, and I now felt that it might not come in time for my trial.

One day, after two weeks of praying over and over again in jail about this dilemma, I was searching the scriptures for answers, and my eye fell on a favorite verse, John 8:32, "And ye shall know the truth, and the truth shall make you free."

I reread that sentence and said the words aloud, " . . . the truth shall make you free!"

I took a sheet from a pad of yellow, lined paper and wrote those six words on it in bold capitals. I found a piece of used gum and stuck this piece of paper to the wall at the foot of the bed so I'd see it every time I climbed in. My bed was in the wall, in an alcove which dovetailed under the bed alcove in the next cell to save space. A small tamper-proof reading light allowed me to read these reassuring words every time I went there to sleep, nap, or read: THE TRUTH SHALL MAKE YOU FREE.

This message from the Apostle John in the New Testament bored into my consciousness, and I experienced a sweet, peaceful feeling that my prayers were being answered and that I was being told how to win my freedom—by telling the truth.

I can honestly say that I was feeling the promptings of the Holy Spirit at that moment in time, and I knew in my heart that I must trust those feelings if I wanted the Lord to help me win my freedom.

If I were to allow my attorneys to plead and argue "diminished capacity," I'd have to tell a whole new string of lies, and I just couldn't do that any more. Not only was my life at stake, but so, possibly, was the life of the man we'll call Agent X, the agent who I suspected was being misled by the FBI.

I now realized that the Lord was pointing the way back to my family. "The truth shall make you free," was an answer to my prayers.

As I have mentioned, time and the answer to a prayer, together, did two things. They not only stiffened my resolve to reject lying about diminished capacity, they gave me the good sense and courage to tell my attorneys everything the moment I got out of jail.

I was waiting and wasting valuable time they so desperately needed simply because I was convinced that every word I told them was being recorded. If the truth were to make me free, it mustn't be shared with those who wanted to put me away for a long prison term.

At my next meeting with the attorneys, one of them said, "What's this really all about? Can you give us some details? Can you give us some help? How can we help you?"

I was paranoid about being monitored and then charged with violating my security agreement, so I told them, "There's a lot more to this, and when I get out of here I'll be able to talk about it. But I can't tell you in here."

They wanted to know what it was of course, but I wouldn't tell them. They were left with no choice but to go ahead and start preparing this diminished capacity thing for the hearing coming up.

It soon became apparent to me that I wasn't going to be rescued in time—if ever. So my decision was that as soon as I got out I would tell my attorneys everything, and repeat it in court at my trial.

After spending five weeks in segregation, I was free at last. That meant I could finally pour out my story, but not at the attorney's office because it was too easy to bug. In fact, someone had already broken into Bill Cummings' office looking for evidence. There will be a description later as to how the $500,000 bond was finally raised to get me out of the Fairfax County jail.

We decided to meet our attorneys in the basement of our church's meetinghouse in McLean, Virginia. I asked my father to quietly contact Bishop Lowe and arrange it.

It was on a Saturday morning and no one would be there. My younger brother Todd and a couple of friends stood guard near the entries, and my father and I met the attorneys in a classroom, in the basement of the church.

I laid out the whole story, and when I was finished, Brent Carruth just looked at me and said, "You're crazy!"

He said, "No jury in the world would believe that story."

I replied, "Whether they believe it or they don't, it's the truth, and I am convinced that telling the truth will make me free. I've prayed long and hard about it, and I've had my answer! So that's what my defense is going to be—the truth!

They said, "Show us some evidence."

I'm sure they didn't believe my story at that time. They were convinced I was making it up, but I responded.

I said, "I have virtually no evidence. I have a telephone number, and if you trace it back all the way to the end, you're going to find the CIA. Plus, I've got a name that was used on a business-card authenticator, and if you trace it back it might also lead to the CIA. With both a phone number and a card leading to the CIA—well, that's something."

I continued. "I also know how to get in touch with these people through the CIA's San Francisco office because I've done it before through Paul Shields of the FBI. If you trace that particular series of calls through the telephone records of the office involved, I think you'll find the CIA again. Finally, I have a transcript of a conversation between my former secretary and an FBI investigator who told her the FBI knew I'd been working for the CIA."

There was a long pause. Finally they said, "It's not enough! There's just nothing tangible to present to a jury."

However, at that point, I think they may have begun to wonder about it all because it made sense even though there was nothing put on the table for the jury to look at.

Brent Carruth added, "If this is the truth, and if you do use it for your defense, you're going to lose. I'm not saying that because I'm not a good lawyer, I'm telling you because the jury can only deal with evidence. You simply don't have enough evidence, while the government has overwhelming evidence against you."

He went on. "They have your statements that you talked to the Soviets, to the KGB. They have your statements that you disclosed information about Agent X. As your attorney, I'm telling you that I can't defend you. I can't guarantee anything with this defense because there just isn't enough evidence."

Then he said, "Here are your odds. If you go in and tell them what you say is the truth, you have an eighty to ninety percent chance of conviction. If they convict you, I can guarantee you'll get forty years to life." He continued. "On the other hand, if we go in with the diminished capacity defense, I can give you an eighty percent chance that I can get you a five-year suspended sentence, with one year of psychiatric care in a mental hospital."

I said, "No. It's not the truth!"

By this time, we'd moved up from the church basement to the foyer and were seated on couches. I sat on one couch and the attorneys were sitting on the other, facing me across the hallway. My dad was slowly pacing back and forth in the space between us. Brent Carruth had spent about fifteen minutes trying to persuade me that it was in my best interest to go with the diminished capacity defense, but I just kept thinking of that piece of yellow paper on the wall of my cell. It's a piece of paper I've saved and will keep forever.

It said, "The truth shall make you free." I believed that. I had faith that it was true, so I was determined to tell the truth even though I knew I was taking a big gamble. If I should lose, I'd have lost while telling the truth, but I wouldn't have lost my self-respect.

If I were to go in and win on the diminished capacity plea, the world would believe, for the rest of my days on this earth, that Craig Smith was some kind of a dingbat. They would believe that Craig Smith really was a spy, not for money but for his own ego.

I couldn't live with that for the rest of my life. I would rather live in jail having told the truth, than live out of jail having lied or prostituted myself to win a false freedom. So I said I wouldn't do it.

Brent Carruth then turned to my father and said, "Please persuade your son that I care about him, and that his life's worth more than going to jail for forty years. I just don't think I can do it. Persuade him to be easy on himself."

Dad looked at me and said, "Son, I can't tell you what to do, but forty years looks scary to me, too."

I didn't hesitate a moment. I didn't stop to weigh forty years against one. I didn't have the slightest doubt what my answer had to be. I said, "Dad, I'm just going to tell the truth, and that's it."

12

My Attorneys Are Selected

When my mother answered the phone on April 4th, 1984, a reporter asked, "Mrs. Smith, how do you feel about your son having been arrested?"

She replied, "I don't know anything about it."

"Well don't you know that your son has been arrested by the FBI in Virginia?"

"No."

"Well can you tell me anything about it?"

"No," my mother said and hung up the phone.

Thus began the bombardment by phone calls, reporters, and camera crews at my parents' door for the next several days. Mom and Dad simply told them, "We don't have any new information yet," and shut the door.

The network TV bureaus and the national wire services were especially persistent. One prominent TV anchorwoman called my father from New York and asked, "Do you know who I am?"

Dad said, "Yes, I watch you all the time."

"Well you won't hang up on me, will you?"

He did hang up because first of all, my parents really didn't know much. Second, what little they did know had to be kept away from the prosecutors and Justice Department attorneys. My parents knew better than to help the government prepare their case against our meager defense.

It annoyed the prosecution that we continued to stonewall the press because for a couple of precious months they couldn't determine where our defense was coming from, and they couldn't take any action necessary to derail it.

The camera crews and reporters were so aggressive that my parents finally called the bishop of their ward who at that time was Lloyd Cooney, former president of KIRO (CBS) Radio and Television in Seattle. They asked him to use his influence to get the media people off their doorstep. This helped, but the media persisted in fanning out and interviewing everyone in the neighborhood.

None of us will ever forget the kind words and loyal support these neighbors gave the Smith family in our darkest hour. They all spoke highly of my family and of Mom and Dad's role as good Christian parents. Of course, that seldom makes the evening news.

It's significant to note that the minute my extended family heard of my arrest, they immediately mobilized for the battle that followed. Not one of them doubted my innocence, though they knew almost nothing of the case. For example, no one in the family ever suggested we call a family meeting or hold a telephone conference to examine the facts or consider my sanity or my motives. We had been taught to trust each other with our lives as our parents and grandparents had taught us by their own example.

My younger brother Todd was quoted in the newspaper as saying, "The government had no idea what they were getting into when they took on the Smith family."

What's more, not one trusted friend of my parents, many of whom had never even known me, ever doubted the validity of my parents' faith in me, nor did they ever fail to trust the Smith family's integrity.

Through all their years of activity in their church, my parents had built a reputation for integrity and good character that now allowed them to call on their friends to help in the fight. None of these good people shrank back or equivocated. No one gave lame excuses. They knew that my parents knew their son was wrongly accused, and offers of help came from almost all of their friends and members of church congregations they had attended in Salt Lake City, Washington, Denver, and in Bellevue.

Church members, including stake presidents, bishops, and former bishops visited me in jail. They brought me little necessities, and took my clothes and laundered them. Most important of all, they gave me hope and courage.

I had always considered myself to be reasonably strong, but the moral and physical support of our family and friends was an overwhelming boost for my morale. It is impossible to imagine what a difference it made when my hopes for CIA intervention turned to doubts and then to despair. I was never, ever allowed to feel I was abandoned.

When my older brother Hy, a pilot for Ozark Airlines, heard of my arrest, he went straight to the airline and requested an indefinite leave of absence to enable him to join me. It was granted, and he was able to help me devise strategy from the very beginning of my jail term.

First, we had the question of accepting the court-appointed attorney, William B. Cummings, of Alexandria, Virginia. Bill Cummings had just entered private practice, having shortly before resigned as a U.S. Attorney. He'd worked on many federal cases as a member of the prosecution team. In fact, he had successfully prosecuted and obtained convictions in the Humphrey-Trong espionage case in the late 1970's.

Initially Hy and I tended to be wary of him. Could he have been planted by the government to complete the bizarre kangaroo court I seemed to be up against?

Bill Cummings was born in New York state and moved to Virginia when he was ten. He told me later that even though he'd always thought of himself as a Virginian, natives don't consider anyone a Virginian who wasn't born there.

In spite of his New York origins, he was the epitome of the consummate Southern gentleman with the soft-spoken poise, manners, and breeding of the South. He was quiet, slow to anger, and came across as charming and gracious to those he met. He was highly respected for his absolute honesty and integrity, and worked extremely well with the legal and judiciary community around Alexandria. Further, he was an expert on Virginia law, and he knew the ropes in both the U.S. district court and the appellate court systems.

It took some time, though, before my family and I decided we could commit my fate to Bill Cummings—or any other court-appointed attorney for that matter. We were concerned that he might be a shill for the government.

He must have sensed our apprehension, especially when I refused, because of my security agreement, to give him any significant details about my case. To overcome our fears, he took the time to telephone my parents, introduce himself, and explain his background.

He said to them, "Mr. and Mrs. Smith, your son is in serious trouble. I have to let you know that there's no question he'll have to serve some time in prison. My job is to reduce that time to the minimum possible."

He went on to compare my case to a signed promissory note when it's introduced as evidence. "He's indicated that he's done these things of his own volition, and the government holds the signed note."

Should we keep Bill Cummings, brilliant, persuasive, gentle—yet government appointed?

We prayed daily for help in this decision and were finally persuaded by promptings and feelings that came as answers to our prayers. Later, we learned how fortunate it was that not only was he selected to defend me, but we didn't dismiss him when we retained our own counsel.

There was a second attorney, a Mormon, who made himself known to us. Out of the blue, my mother got a phone call from Van Nuys, California, a few days after my arrest. A voice said, "I'm Brent Carruth, and I read about your son in the paper. I had occasion to take a deposition from Craig two years ago in Salt Lake City."

He went on, "He impressed me in such a way that I have a feeling that he's innocent of these charges. I thought perhaps I'd call and offer my help. You're going to need assistance in selecting a law firm capable of taking on the U.S. government because there are so few that are qualified to do so." He named a few nationally known firms, some of which we'd already considered.

My mother was somehow inspired to ask, "Well, are you one of these lawyers?"

Brent paused and then replied, "Well, I really don't know whether I am or not. I'd have to talk with Craig and see what this case is all about. But I will confer with him and let you know."

My mother asked, "When could you meet with him?" thinking it would take a month or so to get a Los Angeles attorney to fly to Virginia.

He replied, "I'll be on a plane this afternoon, at my own expense."

After lengthy conversations with Brent Carruth, Hy and I knew that he would be essential to our defense. We learned later that Brent had never told my parents he was a member of our church. They discovered that later and thought that showed real professionalism.

We got to know Brent quite well very early in the case. He told us about how he had grown up in poverty, supporting his mother. He had to turn down a scholarship from Harvard Law School in order to stay home and help his family, but still he graduated with a four point grade average from Loyola University Law School in Los Angeles, and worked for a famous trial lawyer. When his mentor died, Brent took over his practice and has been highly successful.

In contrast to Bill Cummings' strengths, Brent Carruth's greatest contributions to the defense team were his brash tenacity and his belief in my innocence. It became clear that he was not intimidated by governments, courts, or prosecutors, and simply would not give up. Once he was committed, he was indefatigable. There was another side to Brent below the surface. He was one of the kindest persons I've ever met, and he had a delightful sense of humor. He was up-front and wouldn't tolerate waffling or lying.

Left to right: Brent, Craig, Bill.

Bill Cummings' charm, on the other hand, came from his diplomacy and from his friendliness. Bill was tall, lean, and patrician, while Brent came on like a boilermaker. Together, they made a good-guy, bad-guy team.

Someone observed that if Bill Cummings had to go through a brick wall, he'd measure it carefully and then begin surgically removing one brick at a time. On the other hand, Brent Carruth would put his head down and charge the wall without even stopping to find out how thick it was.

A defense team was coming together. It was unfortunate that it took five weeks to get me out of the county jail so we could begin the real investigation which led to proving I had been, in fact, working for the CIA.

MY ATTORNEYS ARE SELECTED

* * * * *

Near the end of my first week in jail, the marshals came for me very early in the morning. It was the day of my indictment hearing in the U.S. District Court in Alexandria, so they allowed me to dress in a suit and tie, then took me to a room where I met my two attorneys. The marshals prepared me and two other prisoners for the ride to the federal courthouse. I was surprised when they didn't put waist chains and leg irons on the three of us, but apparently due to the early hour, they just put our hands forward and placed handcuffs on our wrists.

The other two passengers provided quite a contrast. One was an escaped convict serving multiple life terms for kidnapping, murder, and other serious crimes. He had just shot a marshal while being recaptured. The other was, of all things, the young son of a former deputy director of the CIA. He'd been picked up the night before for drunk driving.

Just as we entered the tree-lined streets of residential Alexandria, I remarked without thinking, "Well it's so early, at least the TV cameras won't be there."

One of the marshals said, "What do you mean TV cameras?"

I replied that every time I got near a courtroom, the TV crews showed up.

The marshal said, "Wait a minute, you're that Smith guy, aren't you? The one accused of espionage?"

"Yes, that's right."

They stopped the car immediately, right in the middle of a middle-class residential area, had the three of us get out on the sidewalk in front of a home at seven o'clock in the morning, and put our waist chains and leg irons on us. It seems they they were not about to let the news media telecast their failure to comply with prisoner-movement procedures.

The young D.W.I. was an even funnier case. Imagine how he must have felt at the prospect of having his famous father see him on the breakfast news for the first time, lined up between a hardened convict and an accused spy—in chains.

When we arrived at the courthouse we discovered I'd been right. There were no television cameras that early. The indictment hearing proceeded, and the findings of the grand jury were read to me and my attorneys by Judge William Bryant.

Federal grand juries conduct their hearings in private and only consider the government's side of the case to determine whether there is enough evidence to establish probable cause for indictment and trial. Later, when I read the transcript of the grand jury's hearing of my case, I realized how one-sided it really had been.

For example, all of the former double agents whose names I'd been authorized by the CIA to give to the Soviets had been retired many years ago and were sitting safely by their fireplaces, watching television. But when a member of the grand jury asked an FBI witness at the hearing, "Have any of the agents who were compromised by the accused been killed or captured?" the prosecutor wouldn't let him answer. That's because the only truthful answer the witness could have given would have been, "No, absolutely not."

Instead, the prosecutor interrupted the witness and had, himself, answered "Not yet."

Such a response was designed to create a picture in the minds of the grand jury of brave American heroes hiding behind trees and rocks in Eastern Europe while Smith was betraying them to the Russians.

At the indictment hearing a plea of not guilty was entered. Initially I was held without bond, and at this hearing the judge would not change the court's position on that. It was only later, during further pretrial hearings, that bond was finally set. Bill Cummings had told me that we could expect the bond to be set as high as $250,000, but it would likely not exceed that. I was devastated when my brother came to the jail and told me the lowest bond the attorneys could get

Judge Bryant to set for me was for $500,000 cash. The government was certainly intent on keeping me in jail until the trial.

A major surprise was when Bill Cummings came to me in jail one day and told me that Judge Bryant would not be hearing my case. "Since he is the senior judge in this district, it's his prerogative to appoint another judge to hear any given case, and he just appointed Judge Richard Williams to hear yours, so that's who we'll be dealing with."

I'd had so many surprises and disappointments by then that my heart sank as I thought of being handed down to some kind of "hanging judge" prepicked by the Justice Department to be sure they got me.

However, Bill said, "Actually, I know them both, and this could be a break in our favor."

He continued. "Judge Bryant is fair but less patient. He might move the case faster than we can prepare. When he's decided where a case is heading, he gets on his horse and goes there. Judge Williams, on the other hand, is equally fair, but in addition he's a very compassionate man."

That was nice to hear, but then he added, "Besides, if you are convicted, Judge Williams would probably tend to give you a lighter sentence. Judge Bryant would throw the book at you." This was before Bill had any information to persuade him of my innocence.

If Judge Richard Williams was a compassionate man, he kept it well hidden during every pretrial hearing we appeared at while I was still in jail. My attorneys offered motion after motion to get a little bit of balance into my case against the government's prosecution juggernaut. "Motion denied!" was about all I heard him say.

Bill Cummings continued to reassure me that Judge William Bryant would probably have been even worse in preliminary hearings. Because he had heard the FBI's case in full before the grand jury, and the evidence on the surface was so damaging, he had seemed intent on wrapping the whole thing up in ninety days at the maximum.

Maybe this was the reason Judge Bryant removed himself from the case and appointed Judge Williams, who later became a real champion of our search for the truth.

My wife and my parents—and I, alone in my jail cell—had all prayed fervently to the Lord, asking Him to soften the hearts of the good people in government.

I'm convinced that Judge Bryant truly is a good man, and his heart was somehow touched to reexamine his direction in my case. I believe that he was inspired to turn it over to a judge who could take a fresh look at it, and be sure that the truth was given every chance to be heard.

Richard Williams, in his middle sixties, was a kindly southern gentleman with a sense of humor and a warm heart. It was only after I got out of jail, when we could present our complete defense, that we felt this warmth for the first time.

We found that once we got past the formalities of the law, Judge Williams was plain-spoken and given to reaching to the nub of the issue. In later hearings and in the trial itself, he and Brent Carruth got along famously because they were on the same wave length.

Once during one of the many pretrial sessions, when the prosecutor was off base and didn't realize that he was, Brent stood up and proceeded to tell a joke right in the middle of the courtroom, in front of the press, spectators, and all.

He said, "Your Honor, the prosecutor here is like a man I knew who had a jumping frog. He kept experimenting on his frog by cutting off one leg at a time. Each time, he'd yell, 'Jump, frog, jump!' " Brent would slam his huge hand on the table with each command. Finally, when all four legs were gone and the frog couldn't move at all when he was yelled at, the man said, 'This frog must be deaf!' Your Honor, that's the same with the prosecutor. He's not getting the point here at all!"

Judge Williams leaned back, swung around in his chair, and laughed until tears rolled down his cheeks. He enjoyed Brent's Abe

Lincoln style, and the two of them shared many jokes and anecdotes throughout the hearings and the trial itself.

Brent had a style and talent for fun that seemed to amuse Williams. The judge came to enjoy having Brent Carruth in his court, and his respect for Bill Cummins was unquestionable. Later this helped to frustrate overly confident prosecutors who took themselves too seriously. All of these things helped our cause.

13

Freed On $500,000 Bond

The momentum of the prosecution gathered, having been triggered by my media-event arrest in April and fueled by Judge Bryant's original determination to start the trial by July of 1984.

Until I was released in mid-May, my attorneys had to work in the dark. Although they tried to convince me to plead not guilty by reason of diminished capacity, I refused, leaving them with little to present the judge at preliminary hearings.

At this point, they gambled. They hinted at putting on a full-blown insanity defense for two secret reasons. First, they wanted to keep the Justice Department's prosecution team off balance and stall for time until I could get out of jail. Second, they wanted the court to pay for a psychological evaluation, mostly to determine just what kind of defendant they had in Richard Craig Smith.

Then a coincidence occurred. Just as they began hinting at insanity, Brent Carruth got a phone call from someone in the Psychology Department at U.C.L.A. telling him that a woman psychologist by the name of Dr. Sherry Skidmore would call him momentarily, and that he should consider her offer of help. Dr. Skidmore did call. She turned out to be one of Los Angeles' leading forensic psychologists, specializing in testing defendants and witnesses, then testifying to the results of her evaluations at their trials like any other expert witness.

Brent wanted to engage her services because I was about to be released from jail, but when he moved for permission to fly me to Los Angeles for testing, it was denied. The idea was so compelling that my attorneys moved for a government psychologist to do the same thing, without my leaving the area. Robert Madsen, one of the nation's foremost forensic-testing psychologists and an employee of the U.S. government, was retained by my attorneys to conduct the testing.

Brent Carruth was convinced that, in spite of Madsen's work, it would be important to fly Sherry Skidmore to Virginia for two days of intensive evaluation in order to compare her findings with those of Madsen. This would help determine if I was telling my attorneys the truth or if I was just a very clever liar, perhaps even a psychopathic liar.

For two full days, Dr. Skidmore put me through a battery of many different tests and interviews. She told my attorneys it was the most exhaustive set of tests for determining personality characteristics she'd ever administered.

In a private meeting with Bill Cummings and Brent Carruth she said, "No matter what the evidence shows, Craig is telling the truth, and you'd better believe him. If ever you think he's not telling the truth, just remember, I've tested him against all of the 'lie scales' known to science, and that's just not the case." She repeated, "He's innocent, and he's telling the truth. In fact, I don't believe he has even the capacity to betray his country. You'd better believe him."

Although I wasn't in the room, some one who was there told me later that Bill turned to Brent and said, "You know, this may be interesting. We may have an innocent man here."

I believe that this was the moment when Bill and Brent began to believe me. It was the first time that they acknowledged that maybe I was innocent. They had been defending a man accused of extremely serious crimes, and they had been struggling against a great deal of circumstantial evidence. Perhaps in their own minds they felt they had been defending a guilty man.

After I had told them repeatedly that I refused to agree to a diminished capacity defense, I'm sure they believed that I thought my story was true. They themselves were not yet convinced of it, at least not all of it.

I can't really say I blame Bill and Brent for being so slow to believe my story at first, even though it would be nearly impossible to fabricate any part of it. It would be improbable that I, let alone my attorneys, could guess just how a Soviet KGB officer like Viktor Okunev would react to an American, whether a traitor or a double agent.

That is why, when Dr. Sherry Skidmore finished her work, she offered to bring in a Soviet defector she knew who was then teaching in the Psychology Department at U.C.L.A. Perhaps his expert opinion would shed additional light on the truthfulness of my story.

His name was Nicolai Kokhlov, and his story is fascinating. He'd been approached many years ago by the CIA while working as a KGB agent in East Berlin. They tried to get him to defect, but he refused at first and then changed his mind.

He agreed to set up a Voice of America broadcast in West Berlin, provided his wife and child in Moscow would be protected by asylum in the U.S. Embassy. Somehow the CIA failed to get to his family before the night of the first broadcast, and the two were later discovered to have died somewhere in Siberia.

Kokhlov was a shattered man and for a time refused to work for the CIA. He was tried in absentia by the Soviets and placed on the KGB's death list. Then he softened and served the CIA with valor in South Viet Nam.

It took two-and-a-half hours to tell my story to Dr. Kokhlov, but when I had finished, Brent asked him one simple question.

"Is Craig telling the truth?"

Dr. Kokhlov replied, "Yes. Totally."

When I came to the part about Danny II in the Honolulu park

saying, "Ken White is in Hong Kong," Dr. Kokhlov, with his many years of experience in both the KGB and the CIA, said, "Ken White wasn't in Hong Kong. Ken White was in trouble."

My attorneys were finally becoming convinced even though they still hadn't been given any tangible "hands-on" evidence. Because of the reliability of these two experts, one in psychology and one who'd been on both sides of the counterintelligence game, they were beginning to believe me now.

From this moment onward, my relationship with Bill and Brent began to be solidified. We proceded with the confidence that perhaps we could prevail over the government prosecutors rather than just hope for the best.

Dr. Sherry Skidmore's report had about twenty pages of detail to support her conclusion that I was programmed from my early years to tell the truth. When we moved to have her testimony and data admitted as evidence at my trial, the prosecutors did all they could to prevent her from appearing. Fortunately, Judge Williams ruled in our favor, and she became a key witness on my behalf, using an overhead projector to explain her written evaluation and conclusions. Her influence on the jury must have been a significant plus for our side.

When I was prevented from traveling to Los Angeles for Dr. Skidmore's evaluation, we used the government's man, Robert Madsen. His report supported Dr. Skidmore's conclusions so well that he was indirectly threatened with the loss of his government job if he so testified. Under these circumstances we couldn't use him at our trial. That was the first of several instances of witness tampering.

If Dr. Skidmore's first phone call to Brent Carruth was just a remarkable coincidence there's still one compelling question: Who or what prompted Dr. Sherry Skidmore to pick up the telephone and offer her expert testing services, via the U.C.L.A. Psychology Department?

I think I know. In fact, I know I know!

* * * * *

After about a week in jail, my bond was set at $500,000 cash to guarantee that I would appear for my trial. Setting the bond that high was ridiculous since I was anxious to be heard before a jury to clear my name and reputation. Leaving the country was an option I'd never considered.

At the same time, we retained two attorneys instead of one, which put an additional financial strain on my family. We had to advance the immediate out-of-pocket costs of their investigation, travel, and expenses. For these reasons, the members of my family all pitched in for the legal costs, and my parents went to work on the telephone, sometimes the clock around, to raise the bond money.

Through the hard work of the attorneys, the cash requirement was modified to include letters of credit and/or deeds to real property. It was a staggering challenge for our family of moderate means to face, having to raise one-half million dollars in only a few days. The Smiths may be tenacious fighters, but we are not millionaires.

It took my parents three solid weeks to get the right combination of friends and relatives to complete the total. Included were irrevocable letters of credit issued by banks who would pay the face amount to the court if I didn't show up for my own trial.

The real property was quite a different matter. The court allowed up to half the bond to be secured, not just by notes and second mortgages on real property, but by deeds backed by current appraisals. It normally takes from three weeks to three months to get a property appraisal, and my family was fighting for every single day they could save, knowing that my defense team was stymied until I could be freed on bond. To make matters even worse, the court would only agree to value each deed at fifty percent of the appraised equity, which means, for example, that a family member's deed to their $180,000 home, with a $100,000 mortgage, would only count for one-half of $80,000, or $40,000.

Finally a package was arranged with commitments from a half-dozen relatives and friends who held deeds to a number of properties. These, along with the required bank letters of credit, exceeded the required total.

Although some were family members, many of these people didn't even know me because I'd lived a life of professional obscurity for the most part. It was the unimpeachable character and honesty of my parents that raised this massive bond for me. These people knew that if Dad said I'd be there for my trial, I'd be there—period.

Each one of them voluntarily staked everything he or she owned upon my parents reputation and on their relationship with their son. If I'd fled the country, the court would have taken these peoples' homes. My parents' spent their lifetime building their character and reputation. This became their statement, attested to by loyal friends and their extended family. There is no way I can hope to repay such loyalty and devotion.

The bond amount was finally raised, but little did Dad know then that the job was only half finished. The court had all the deeds and appraisals, and it seemed that all there was left to do was have a bank issue the letters of credit. It was not to be that simple.

One television station in Salt Lake City was so intent on identifying anyone who offered assistance that every time we thought we had a bank ready to go, this station threatened massive publicity about "helping a spy escape from prison and flee the country." They even suggested that the Mormon Church itself might be offering help. That was patently false.

We finally had to go to another state, with Brent's assistance, to find the bank that eventually issued the documents.

Word of the agonizing delays would reach me in jail.

"Just a couple more days," or "Just three more days."

The vindictive actions of this TV channel delayed my release by at least ten days while I rode an emotional roller coaster on each turn of events. Finally, on the 8th day of May, 1984, a jailer came to my cell and told me I was to be released that day. After breathing nothing but "processed" air for five weeks, I was finally going to taste pure, sweet, fresh air again.

I was taken in my prison overalls down to the clothing area for the final time, given my street clothes, handcuffed, and taken in the marshal's car to the now familiar U.S. courthouse in Alexandria. I was met by Bill Cummings and my brother Hy. There I signed the necessary papers agreeing to the terms of my release, to stay in the area and phone the marshals every day. Hy had brought a change of clothes and a razor, so we stopped in the men's washroom for a change and a shave. My brother pinned to my lapel a yellow flower tied with a yellow ribbon. That gesture was typical of Hy—and all my family, for that matter.

We went outside the courthouse, worked our way through a tangle of reporters, and went around a corner in the direction of Bill's office. It was there that I allowed myself to believe it was true. I was free for the first time in five weeks.

Until then, the events of that day had been like all the other countless trips to the courthouse, from the inside of the prison garage to the inside of the courthouse garage—not ever really being allowed to breathe free air. The rush that finally hit me as we stood on that sidewalk was overwhelming. It was euphoria.

I'd experienced this feeling once before, about ten days into my jail experience, when I got my first Hershey bar. I know it sounds silly, but when I was first allowed to buy a Hershey bar from the commissary jailer, I just held it and looked at it. Now, standing on that sidewalk, I was feeling that same wild sensation of gratitude for the freedom we all take for granted in our daily lives.

* * * * *

Since I was not permitted to return to Bellevue, we found an inexpensive hotel apartment for me and any of the family who took turns staying with me. It was situated in a run-down section of Alexandria and was euphemistically called the "Presidential Gardens."

My father arrived the day I got out of jail, and Hy left to go back to his job as airline pilot. For five weeks my older brother had been constantly available to me, even if it was outside the prison bars. My younger brother Todd, still in college, also arrived and stayed from May until July when I was finally allowed to return to Bellevue to await my trial.

We needed the space in the Presidential Gardens to house the Smiths as they came and went. Their physical and moral support meant more than I can ever express.

A small army of people throughout the nation deserve my praise and thanks for their continuing vigil, their faithfulness, and their prayers on my behalf. As the news spread throughout the U.S., wherever we had family and friends, they prayed not only for me, but for Judge Williams and other "good people in government" to make right decisions.

Back in Alexandria at the Presidential Gardens, at Bill Cummings' office, even in private homes, events were steamrolling forward. The serious work on my defense could go ahead for the first time.

My father and brothers stayed close to me for companionship, moral support, and for another more compelling reason; I was no longer protected by a jail cell.

We felt that after I ended my security silence, as word would reach the FBI and CIA about our investigative breakthroughs, certain individuals might reach the point where they could no longer stand up to the heat and light of the truth. Sooner or later, someone might be tempted to silence me another way.

There was good reason to be mindful of such a possibility. By this time my attorney's office and our apartment at the Gardens had been broken into, most likely in an attempt to find anything that could be used to slow us down. We didn't know where they would stop. My family felt I could benefit from their protection, and they took action accordingly.

14

The Search For The Truth

Returning to the events in the church basement, I had revealed the full CIA story to my attorneys for the first time on May 12, 1984.

After Brent Carruth said, "You're crazy!" he added, "Is that all you can give us?"

I'm sure they were expecting me to produce a suitcase full of evidence. I told them, "The evidence is all out there somewhere. We just have to go out and get it."

There was only one place to start, and that was Ken White's hellophone number. I'd hidden it so well at home my wife Susan couldn't find it at first. After telling her where to look for it among my coded papers, she succeeded, and Dad and Todd rushed to the Library of Congress and spent two days going through special reverse directories until they found it.

It was listed as belonging to CMI Investment Co. in Honolulu, the same name that was on the authenticator card shown to me. That was Richard P. Cavannaugh's business card. This was a major breakthrough.

At that time we didn't know who Richard P. Cavannaugh was. Until then it was just a name I'd been shown on a business card, first by Ken White and then by Danny II in a Honolulu park.

We were convinced we had to act swiftly because the government could have swept away the trail. It is possible it did so a few days later as stories about CMI Investment Co., Bishop-Baldwin, and the CIA began to surface in a separate but parallel case in Hawaii.

To substantiate our findings even further, we retained a former investigator for the FBI and the National Park Service, Peter Silvain, to independently trace the same number. He came up with the same name, "CMI Investment Co.," so now we had an expert witness.

This was still before Dr. Sherry Skidmore's evaluation. Up to this moment Bill and Brent had to consider the possibility that I could have been fabricating the whole thing. In fact, for a few days after the church basement meeting, the attorneys were still trying to sell us on the diminished capacity defense, and Dad was still on the fence.

Now we had our first two thin threads of evidence, a phone number and a business card, knotted together, at least. While it still didn't tie in the CIA, it did get our attorneys' attention. Shortly thereafter Dr. Skidmore's evaluation convinced them of two things. First, we had to go for the truth, and second, my life could be in danger as the truth began to rattle cages within the U.S. government.

I persuaded them that the only sure way to buy some real life insurance at this point was to tell my story to the press and get it printed in detail on page one. Then if any harm did come to me, the finger would point to the people in the Agency, thus slowing them down from any decision to silence me through other means.

We weighed the consequences and deliberated for hours over this "insurance policy" plan because we could be making the mistake of alerting the government as to how much we knew. The federal government has enormous powers at its disposal when it comes to sweeping evidence under the rug. As long as we worked secretly, we would stand a better chance of assembling the proof we needed before they could hide it from us. Finally, we decided to break the story openly to the press because without my being alive, the evidence would be worthless anyway.

After I got out of jail, I read the newspaper accounts of my arrest for the first time, since no papers were allowed to reach me inside. One reporter, Lena Sun, covering the Alexandria court circuit for the Washington Post, had done a stand-out job of writing a balanced analysis of the case. She was the most objective of all we read, so we selected her for our bombshell news release. We called her and said, "Lena, we're going to break this story to you. Can you come out immediately?"

We met Lena in Bill Cummings' office in Alexandria. We suspected that his office was bugged by the government, and chose it for this interview for that reason. We wanted them to know we were going public this time, so it didn't matter if they listened in or not.

For two hours, I laid out the whole story and answered Lena's questions with Bill and Brent present. Then it was time to take Brent out to the airport to catch his plane home. He'd been with us for two weeks this time. We invited Lena to ride out with us so she could finish the interview. Before we left, she phoned her copy desk. Lena and her copy editor worked under the famous Bob Woodward who broke the Nixon Watergate story and co-authored "All the President's Men."

I overheard her say to her editor, "You'd better hold the press and give me a lot more space." Then she added, "And tell Bob he was right."

When we got into the car, I asked Lena what she meant by her last comment, and she said, "Woodward thought this whole thing was fishy all along, and he told me right from the beginning that the CIA was messed up in it somehow."

I was amused but not particularly surprised to learn that the prestigious Washington Post had seen through the charade of my arrest at the time it had happened. They had sensed something was wrong. The government just doesn't do it the way it was done in my case. It looked too much like a cover-up of some kind.

Lena's story broke the next day, with the headline, "Accused Spy Tells of Links with CIA, Contacts in Tokyo."

The whole world read that day:

"Accused spy Richard Craig Smith says he passed on military secrets to a Soviet KGB officer in Japan as part of a clandestine operation directed by the Central Intelligence Agency and designed to infiltrate Soviet Intelligence. . . ."

Then Lena ended her story with a final quote from me:

"When he realized the operation was apparently over, Smith says, 'I was just heartbroken. They were throwing away an opportunity, and not only were they throwing it in the trash can, they were picking up the can and hitting me with it.'"

Two days later we knew that our decision to go public immediately was an inspired one. Just forty-eight hours after Lena's article broke in the Washington Post, my brother Hy was watching the ABC Evening News in his home in St. Louis Missouri. Peter Jennings broke a story that the CIA was involved with a crumbling real estate firm in Honolulu known both as Bishop, Baldwin, Rewald, Dillingham and Wong, and also as CMI Investment Co. He phoned us immediately with this information, and we realized that if we hadn't gone public two days earlier, it could have looked as though we'd picked up the story ourselves and tried to ride its coattails. Even though the name "CMI Investment Co." and its phone number didn't get into Lena's article, we had given both to her. That was a matter of record in her notes.

After two more in-depth reports by Jennings on the CIA's embarrassment over Bishop-Baldwin, he suddenly dropped the issue and almost nothing was reported on it. Because of subsequent conflicts between ABC News and the CIA, I feel strongly that Jennings was threatened with his job if he persisted. I also suspect that pressure came down on the executives of the network from the federal government in terms of FCC broadcast licenses and other privileges.

In any case, we now had solid verification of the CIA connection with both Bishop-Baldwin and CMI Investment Co. and positive proof that my contact phone was in a CIA office. My two attorneys were growing optimistic, because for the first time, even though it was still little to go on, they had solid evidence.

Realizing how perishable these leads were, Brent Carruth, by then in Los Angeles, got on the next plane for Honolulu. He walked into the office of the newly appointed trustee for the bankrupt Bishop-Baldwin real estate firm mentioned in the Jennings news program. He arrived at an early hour, seven o'clock in the morning, before any of the executives had come in.

The only person there was a young clerk. He said to her, "I'm an officer of the court, and I want a copy of all the financial records of Bishop-Baldwin."

This young girl, perhaps a bit naive, replied that he could have the printout but said he would have to pay for the computer time.

Brent gladly paid cash, and walked out with an armload of dynamite which would prove once and for all the CIA connection to Bishop-Baldwin and CMI.

It was a serious mistake for the CIA to leave those sensitive computer files unguarded, but somehow they did.

* * * * *

Armed with document after document to prove our CIA story, our attorneys could now go into pretrial conferences with a whole new defense. They now had seen the evidence that I told them they would find if they would just go out and look for it.

They used this evidence to change the tide of events which had been running against us.

In the early hearings before Judge Bryant and Judge Williams, my attorneys were, in essence, marking time. They could present no real defense because they didn't have one. They hinted at insanity while offering motion after routine motion, such as a motion to change venue to Seattle, for example.

Both judges had been presented such a neat, cut-and-dried case by the prosecution that they just wanted to get on with it and wrap up an obvious conviction of a confessed spy.

One day I'd been brought in from the county jail to hear my attorneys argue a simple motion that was carefully prepared and professionally presented. Judge Williams had just taken over the case and sat in stony silence in his chair, seemingly paying little attention to them. Then he picked up a typed paper he'd brought in with him and read his rejection of the motion, a decision that had obviously been made before the hearing ever started.

My father and others were furious, believing that all of the decisions were predetermined and that I had no chance of getting any fair rulings.

Some hearings were even worse, and we were getting slam-dunked by the prosecution every time we turned around. Both judges continued to refuse to accept the argument that there was evidence out there that might be obtainable.

After I had convinced Brent Carruth and Bill Cummings that I really was innocent and that we really did have a case, we went to Judge Williams "in camera," privately, and explained what our defense was going to be. We said that the government had documents that we believed would support what I was saying, and we asked the judge to help us under Rule 16, the Evidentiary Discovery Rule, to force the government to turn over such documents.

At that point Judge Williams' attitude toward me began to change. Until that time his feeling seemed to be that the Justice Department wouldn't have brought Smith in here if he weren't guilty, but now the judge was proving to really be a man of integrity because he was willing to give me a fair shot at doing what I said I could do.

He asked me why we didn't offer this defense before, and I told him the truth—that I didn't even dare tell my own counsel in jail because I didn't trust the government not to monitor our conversations, and I felt I was still under my security agreement.

Brent was back in Virginia with a pile of documents from Honolulu which he'd studied and found to be full of evidence connecting CMI Investment Co. and Bishop-Baldwin to the CIA.

Brent's skill and experience told him that it would be more convincing if, rather than just producing these documents, we could get the government to lie about their existence. Consequently, for the next three or four hearings, Brent would keep the evidence hidden away and just ask the judge to ask the prosecutor for each document by name under Discovery Rule 16. The prosecutor would turn to the CIA people who would tell him that such a document didn't exist, or if it did, it didn't contain any reference to the CIA. This was repeated several times.

Then we'd meet with the judge "in camera" and produce copies of these same documents. At the next hearing, when the prosecutor was confronted with copies of the documents themselves, he'd go back to the CIA, and ask "What about these?" Each time, the CIA would offer some weak excuse.

Thus the government was forced again and again to admit it was being less than forthright, and its case was becoming increasingly convoluted and deceptive. Judge Williams grew more impressed with what we were able to establish and more irritated at the prosecutors and their CIA clients.

The judge began to trust and believe in the possible credibility of our story. I can't say that he jumped onto our bandwagon all at once, but I believe he redoubled his commitment to us and to himself to provide me every opportunity to tell the truth.

* * * * *

The central figure of Peter Jennings' ABC Evening News reports on the Bishop-Baldwin connection was Ronald Rewald, the key player in Bishop, Baldwin, Rewald, Dillingham and Wong. He'd been jailed in Honolulu, having been accused of nearly one hundred counts of fraud in swindling four hundred investors out of twenty-two million dollars. He's currently serving sentences totaling eighty years.

On national network television news, Rewald claimed he was an agent for the CIA and was just following orders. The CIA denied this just as they were denying my connection to them or to their front companies. They did admit having a "slight connection" to Bishop-Baldwin, however.

As soon as Rewald was out on bail, Brent Carruth contacted him and Mr. Rewald basically substantiated what I was saying. As a principal of Bishop-Baldwin he had been instructed by the CIA to set up CMI Investment Co. in order to provide the telephone linkage between Charles Richardson/Richard Cavannaugh and his agents. As earlier noted, it was this Richardson/Cavannaugh who told me, in a phone call from the CIA's San Francisco office, to "keep your (deleted) mouth shut!" This same Richardson/Cavannaugh was president of CMI Investment Co., the paper company that tied his network of agents together. For the first time, we had proof of Richard P. Cavannaugh's real name: Charles L. Richardson, and all we had to do to get it was phone Ron Rewald and ask him.

Mr. Rewald then said, "I have a lot of papers that may be helpful to you."

Subsequently he made available to us a large number of documents that the government didn't know he had, and many of them showed the direct connection between his former companies and the CIA. Apparently he had taken action to protect that information by removing it from his offices, thus insuring that these papers would not be purged in the event of midnight CIA raids on Bishop-Baldwin files.

Again using Rule 16, we would ask the court to require the government to produce certain papers. The CIA would tell the prosecutors there were no such documents. Then we'd go into chambers with the judge, show him our copies, and at the next hearing the government would have to admit they had not been forthright once again. This was repeated a number of times.

Judge Williams began to lose patience with the government's stonewalling, and by now the government prosecutors realized that we were stockpiling more and more evidence damaging to their case. They were more determined than ever to win a conviction and get me put away and silenced for forty years or more.

Their answer was to enter a motion to invoke CIPA. CIPA stands for the Classified Information Procedures Act enacted by Congress which allows the government to classify or reclassify—and thereby quash—any evidence which they feel endangers national security. It's an enormously powerful weapon and should never be used unfairly by a just and lawful government. However, no one seeking to sweep their dirt under the rug is very concerned about unfair, just, or lawful.

Our attorneys argued vigorously against the government motion to seal the evidence we'd fought so hard to produce, and the judge, after hearing considerable argument, ruled against the government, denying their motion.

In strong, unequivocal language, he reiterated the constitutional right to a fair trial and he issued an order indicating that the evidence that he had reviewed was, in his opinion, relevant and admissible, even essential to a fair trial.

He added, "The government is wrong to think that they can invoke the Classified Information Procedures Act to disallow this evidence when there is such a critical constitutional issue here."

One can imagine why the government is generally confident of winning cases involving national security, but in this case there were absolutely no security issues in any of the documents we unearthed. They only damaged the credibility of certain government agencies.

There's little wonder that the government, up to this time in its entire history, had won every single espionage case that ever went to a jury. Prior to my case, according to exhaustive reviews of case law, only two defendants charged with treason ever won their cases, but neither went to a jury trial. One successfully claimed diplomatic immunity and the other was plea-bargained.

In my case the government was attempting to take unfair advantage of me and exercise unrighteous dominion in pursuing its aims.

In any case, Judge Richard Williams' decision against the government was a major turning point in our defense, and we saw his courage and integrity at its finest.

15

The Fight To Have The Truth Admitted

The tide had turned, and we had won our first decision against the United States government. We were delighted, but guardedly so, because we knew the government had the right to appeal the judge's order against them. As expected, an appeal was quickly filed with the Fourth Circuit Court of Appeals in nearby Richmond, Virginia, in July of 1984.

The appeal forced a continuance of my trial and an indefinite new trial date. My attorneys estimated the appeal would mean as much as a four-month delay from the original July date in 1984.

Prepared for the worst even then, I recall hoping that the delay would take six months rather than four. In case anything went wrong at the trial, I could spend at least one more traditional Christmas with my family. However, in November 1984, right on schedule, we won our appeal.

The Fourth Circuit Court of Appeals upheld Judge Williams' order in the same strong language. The three senior judges, out of a total of twelve in the Fourth Circuit, heard arguments from both sides and upheld the order from the lower court, saying in effect that it was highly unusual for the government to submit such an appeal when the evidence was clearly relevant, and more importantly, admissible under the provisions of the constitution.

The decision was unanimously approved by all three senior judges, and the opinion was written by the senior judge of the panel. We'd won again.

The government, however, was not willing to accept the decision handed down by the panel of the three senior judges of the Fourth Circuit. They were prepared to take their appeal all the way to the Supreme Court if they had to.

Accordingly, within the time allotted, they appealed the decision of this three-judge panel and demanded that the issue be heard by all twelve judges of the circuit "en banc." Legal authorities on federal appeals tell us that it was ludicrous to appeal from such a strong, unanimous opinion, and such an action was virtually unprecedented. It was a slap in the faces of those three senior judges. "En banc" appeals are customarily heard only if one of the three judges writes a strong or convincing dissent. It had almost never happened before, but the steam-roller rolled on. The government had to put me away now.

Consequently, after more than an entire year's delay by the government, my two attorneys went to Richmond for the second time and argued our case against the government's second appeal.

There was a humorous note on the proceedings in Richmond; during oral arguments one day, one of the old chandeliers in the courtroom started smoking and caught on fire. One of the twelve judges was overheard to say, "It's probably a CIA bug."

With an even number of judges casting votes, a tie, six votes to six, would have let us win again. My family and I had our hopes built up that the full court would vote to agree with the previous two decisions to admit the evidence in spite of CIPA. I was permitted to wait nervously for the twelve judges' decision in Bellevue, Washington.

When the first postponement had been announced in early July 1984, Judge Williams granted a motion that I be allowed to go home to my family. My challenge was to try to put my life into some semblance of order, pending a later trial date. I was still required to phone the marshals each day, and surveillance continued to plague us.

After living in my parents' home through many months of uncertainty, we finally moved into a small rental house about a mile away, sent the older children back to their same schools again, and waited.

When the news came in November of 1984 that the three judge panel had sustained Judge Williams' order, we thought we were going to have a speedy trial with hundreds of pages of evidence proving my CIA connection. Our frustration, however, was further intensified when we got word from Alexandria that the government had appealed to all twelve judges en banc, and we had no idea how long this would drag out.

As a result, it was difficult trying to put my life back together until after the trial. I held a number of jobs in an effort to provide some income for the family. For a few months I drove a bread truck for a family in our church who owned a bakery. I worked as a night clerk at a motel owned by another family and free-lanced as a consultant to a newly created internationally oriented office and secretarial service for Pacific Rim companies.

None of these jobs led anywhere and we all knew they were only temporary. The employers did all they could to demonstrate their faith in me. They trusted me with everything they had— their trucks, their merchandise, their property, even their cash. I was grateful to be back in the work force.

It was fruitless to send out resumes or to interview for long-term career positions. It was possible that there would be no long term because of the uncertainty of the date or outcome of the trial that would inevitably take place.

Any serious employer was in a difficult position. Anyone looking across his desk at an individual accused of being a traitor to his country would find it impossible even to discuss a career of any kind.

He could be kind and sympathetic to my plight, but underneath, subconsciously, there would always be the nagging question, "Did he or didn't he?"

I often felt that casual conversations with friends were backdropped by the unspoken feeling of wondering, "Could he have really done this?" Every patriotic American has been programmed to believe that his government is a just government. Perhaps it is the only country in the entire world to attain true "liberty and justice for all."

The FBI, especially, is equated by most people with God, mother, and apple pie. It doesn't make mistakes of this enormity. Besides, all the FBI had to do was phone the CIA and check out my story.

I finally became convinced that self-employment was the only way to provide a living for my family for what turned out to be another twelve months before my trial finally took place. That was in the spring of 1985, nine months after I'd returned to Bellevue and taken a succession of temporary positions.

In the early summer of 1985 an opportunity surfaced that suited my talents well. I joined a small advertising agency and free-lanced on my own for nearly a year. I had some expertise in this area, and I began to see a future for myself in helping people promote their message by presenting products and services in the competitive heat of the market place.

I was earning a living for a change, and I'd found a niche that was compatible with my situation. I was determined to make the most of every day.

I've always considered myself to be very positive, and I've trusted in God to send me no test or trial that was impossible to endure. It seemed that things, for the first time in a long time, were beginning to come together somewhat. My wife and my children enjoyed good health and positive attitudes. Most important of all, we were together. I had two of the world's finest people serving as my attorneys. We were still gathering evidence from sources all over the map. My own health was excellent, and my goals for myself and my family never wavered. I knew who I was. I knew where I was going.

The happiest development of all was Susan's attitude. For almost two years she had endured uncompromising stress, and she had to trust in me, in the attorneys, and in the Lord when she was still not permitted to know the details.

Although she was strong, even saints are subjected to the wearing down process. Day after day, week after week, she was called upon to trust, while almost every institution in the entire world—government, press, and public opinion, cried "Guilty!"

Whether or not she ever wavered, only she will know. I never doubted her steadfastness though I'm certain her faith was tried many times.

When I left her to go and face the FBI, knowing that I might be arrested, I told her, "No matter what happens, no matter what I'm accused of, I haven't done anything wrong, and the evidence will bear me out and prove me right."

Many a husband has said these words, and many a wife has trusted. Susan was asked to meet the supreme test of loyalty, and she never faltered.

It isn't hard to imagine how a woman would feel if her husband said, "Trust me, even though I can't tell you what I've done." However, it must have been even more frightening when she first read his story in the newspapers and then heard the rest of the world claim that he fabricated the story out of sheer desperation.

On the other hand, Judge Richard Williams' eyes had seen the proof to the contrary. He had seen hundreds of pages of government documents proving the CIA's involvement as I had claimed, and he'd ruled that this body of evidence was not only relevant and admissible to my trial, it was essential. That was the turning point for Susan. Not for her level of trust, but for her attitude. Now that an impartial federal judge had seen the evidence that her husband was telling the truth, her attitude became more confident and positive because for the first time, someone she could trust had seen the proof. It told the whole world what she already knew but couldn't prove.

It made a great difference. Now she could prepare for the worst. No matter how much we both loved our country, Susan could prepare to raise our children alone if need be, knowing that I was the victim of some kind of savage crossfire within our government. In fact she did such a good job of preparing her attitude for the worst, I actually felt sometimes I was in the way.

* * * * *

We waited nearly two years for a trial date to be set. The original date was to have been in July of 1984, only four months after my arrest in April. The government's July appeal to the Fourth Circuit was denied in November, four months later. Then the government's "en banc" appeal took another sixteen months to be decided.

The anguish of two long years of waiting in limbo was moderated by the Apostle John's admonition, "Know the truth, and the truth shall make you free." My faith in God's protective hand never wavered.

At last the full court decision was announced. They overturned both the three-judge panel and Judge Richard Williams!

In March of 1986, the twelve judges of the Fourth Circuit Court of Appeals ruled in favor of the government invoking CIPA, by a vote of seven to five. We were shocked at this unexpected outcome. We didn't know what had caused the reversal, but it was a devastating turn of events for us.

All our evidence was quashed. Our defense was suddenly toothless. We had to go into court in thirty days with none of the documentation that proved I was telling the truth.

We needed a miracle. Would God send one to us?

16

Preparing For The Trial

We had just thirty days before my trial was to begin on Monday, April 7th, 1986. There were only four weeks to reorganize our defense, appear at pretrial conferences, prepare our witnesses, arrange for their travel to Alexandria, Virginia, and hold a one day dress rehearsal. All this with our documentary proof of my innocence — hundreds of pages of government communications—barred from my trial.

Instead of a dress rehearsal they call it a "mock trial," and it's held for several reasons. Most importantly it gives us a chance to try out our defense on a mock jury of people off the street and train our witnesses in what to expect from the attorneys, especially the prosecution.

Conducting mock trials is a very specialized field, and we were fortunate to have a coach who had spent nearly two years following my case and preparing for this final thrust. Donna Siers held a Master's Degree in Forensic Communications and was an expert in her field.

In June of 1984, when we thought the trial was going to be in July, Bill Cummings' wife and secretary, Diane, called the office of the famous trial lawyer F. Lee Bailey and asked them for references of specialists in jury selection and witness preparation. They suggested a firm in Iowa, who in turn referred us, because of our limited budget, to Donna Siers who was quite new but evidenced strong capabilities.

By then our defense team consisted of our two attorneys, Bill Cummings and Brent Carruth, Dr. Sherry Skidmore, Dr. Joseph Smith, Peter Silvain, and now Donna Siers—all committed to the common goal of defending an innocent victim of government crossfire.

Defense team. Left to right: (back row) David (associate of Mr. Cummings), Bill Cummings, Craig, Brent Carruth, Peter Silvain (investigator); (front row) Donna Siers, Dr. Sherry Skidmore (testing psychologist), Dr. Joseph Smith.

A week before the real trial on a Saturday, Donna conducted the mock trial in front of twelve "jurors" who were friends or acquaintances of the Cummings, and who volunteered the day for a token honorarium. Bill presented the prosecution's case, and the attorneys called a number of key witnesses to be examined and cross-examined. After each witness, the "jurors" filled out a questionaire.

Was this witness credible? Do you believe his/her story? Did the "prosecutor's" cross-examination undermine your belief in the witness?

At the end of the "trial," each of three groups of four "jurors" sat in a private room around a tape recorder and deliberated. In the aggregate, they voted eleven to one for acquittal. One car salesman, a former veteran, felt he couldn't vote against the FBI.

This was vital information, as Donna was to be our key advisor during jury selection, sitting next to our attorneys and helping them determine the potential of the prospective jurors. She had one other job besides the mock trial and jury selection, witness preparation. She prepared us to talk effectively to the jury without fear, nervousness, or frustration. She helped us to be our most believable selves, to understand procedure and not to be caught off guard. She made a priceless contribution in all three areas as was evidenced later during the trial itself.

There were pretrial conferences for a day-and-a-half where all the ground rules were established. During these sessions the judge explained how he proposed to instruct the jury, both at the opening and closing of the trial itself. He accepted input from both sides and then negotiated his final instructions. The CIPA matters were discussed, and the judge and both attorneys agreed as to what would be permitted and what would be barred. Although the pretrial conferences were held in open court, those without security clearances, both public and press, were excused from the CIPA discussions.

Finally, "voir dire," the process of questioning jurors, was discussed. Judge Williams announced that the attorneys would not be allowed to ask questions, but they would submit a general list from which only he would choose questions such as, "Are you a veteran?" "Are you related to an employee of the CIA or FBI?" or "Have you read about this case?"

There was one final bit of drama, before the trial, that ultimately made a huge difference in our case, but it had the effect of a roller coaster. It concerned certain additional documents we got from Ronald Rewald pertaining to the CIA and Bishop-Baldwin which were also ruled classified under CIPA during Rewald's trial in August of 1985.

Rewald was the key figure of Bishop, Baldwin, Rewald, Dillingham and Wong—and CMI Investment Co. (Richardson/Cavannaugh's "paper" company). He was prosecuted and convicted in U.S. District Court in Honolulu on nearly one hundred counts of fraud when four hundred investors lost twenty-two million dollars in the collapse of this investment company, which was actually a front for the CIA's Pacific operations. Rewald claimed he was employed by the CIA, under Charles L. Richardson/Richard P. Cavannaugh, of the CIA's San Francisco office.

Donna Siers, who stayed on our team for twenty-two months waiting for my trial, decided to go to Honolulu for Rewald's trial, to learn anything which might help our cause. After she conducted the mock trial many months later, we were all in a strategy meeting to beef up our defense in the weak areas revealed by our mock jury's reactions. Donna remembered hearing a rumor from someone on Rewald's defense team who had mentioned that some documents had been declassified now that his trial was over and he was in jail. They had only been classified in order to prevent Rewald's access to them during his trial—to prevent the jury from hearing the truth.

Apparently it hadn't occurred to anyone on that case that these documents might help Craig Smith, so why not declassify them since Rewald's trial was over?

Brent immediately filed a request for these files, and the prosecution, during oral arguments over this request, resorted to the most specious of reasoning to try again to block us.

Under court order the chief prosecutor, Joseph Aronica, had brought these papers to the courtroom in a carton and set the box on the table. Then he argued that the Fourth Circuit Court of Appeals' ruling of inadmissibility still applied to them. Aronica argued that the Fourth Circuit's final ruling was they were inadmissible because they were classified, and that the act of declassifying them did not suddenly make them admissible. That would take a separate order from the Fourth Circuit, he argued.

Judge Williams told the prosecutor, "Nonsense, give the documents to them."

The prosecution's team slowly, reluctantly got up out of their chairs and carried the box over to our table.

One other incident was very disturbing to the prosecution team. When we first received additional documents from Ron Rewald, we discovered the name "Mr. Ishida" on one page.

We showed it to Judge Williams, and he took great delight in asking the prosecution if the name "Ishida" was found anywhere on any document pertaining to Bishop-Baldwin.

They replied, "No."

The judge said, "Well, I'm holding a memo in my hand that clearly refers to a Mr. Ishida. And if I can find it, why can't you?"

We took the box and examined the contents carefully, and it was all right there. We were back in business, with dozens of pertinent documents, a few of which were new to us and especially useful to our cause. Thanks to Donna's good detective work, we were right back in the race.

However, we failed again to reckon with the U.S. government's obsession with eradicating any and all evidence we could use in my defense. On Sunday night, the night before the trial was to begin, we were told that the government's attorneys had persuaded the Fourth Circuit to issue a last minute order holding this box of documents to be inadmissible under their previous CIPA decision.

As far as tangible, documented evidence was concerned, we were back to square one.

The score now read: Lions one hundred. Christians zero.

17

The Trial Begins

On Monday, April 7th, 1986, at nine o'clock in the morning, the case of the United States of America vs. Richard Craig Smith was finally opened in U.S. District Court in Alexandria, Virginia, before Judge Richard L. Williams. I was charged by the FBI and the Justice Department with two counts of espionage against the U.S., one count of conspiracy, and two counts of passing U.S. government secrets to the Soviet Union.

The night before, the government had succeeded again in quashing our hard-won documentary evidence supporting my true story of having been in the employ and under the total control of the Central Intelligence Agency while winning the confidence of the KGB's third-highest-ranking officer in the Far East, Asia, Viktor Okunev.

* * * * *

Monday was a bright spring day in Alexandria and I was really looking forward to telling my story to a jury of my peers at long last.

I no longer felt the nervousness I had experienced while on the stand in procedural hearings over the past twenty-four months. Then I found myself emotionally tense, pleading for my life. Now I felt calm and prepared.

We met that morning in Bill Cummings' office, three blocks from the courthouse. We joined together in prayer, Mormon church members and non-members alike, to invoke God's blessing on the trial, and I came away feeling spiritually refreshed and eager to get on with it.

The entire defense team was together now: attorneys Bill Cummings and Brent Carruth, Dr. Sherry Skidmore, Dr. Joseph Smith, Donna Siers, Peter Silvain—as well as my parents, Hyrum and Dorothy Smith, three of my brothers, Hy, Lane and Todd, my sister Terry, and Susan's father, Mitchell Woods, who had flown in from Denver to support Susan while I was absorbed in preparation that final week.

Some of our witnesses had begun to arrive, including Fred Schwendiman, Dad's long-ago missionary companion and a Vice President of Brigham Young University, "Uncle Fred" to my family all these years. Fred had to fly home from Jerusalem where he'd been supervising the installation of the BYU study facility there. Always a man who goes the extra mile, he flew all the way to Salt Lake City to receive a blessing from my cousin, M. Russell Ballard, a Latter-day Saint General Authority. Then he flew to Alexandria to be with us and extend the blessing from a respected church leader to us individually.

My Dad asked Fred to be our spiritual leader, and the two of them gave blessings to those who asked for them. That included Dr. Sherry Skidmore, a devout Seventh-day Adventist.

We all walked the three blocks together to the courthouse, and used an alley entrance to avoid the crowds of newspeople. We entered the courtroom and took our seats while Judge Williams opened with the selection of the jury from the ninety-six candidates called. Although I sat with my two attorneys at the defense table, I had the oddest sensation that it wasn't I who stood on trial. I seemed to be a fascinated observer looking in on the proceedings.

The selection of the jury moved quickly as it does in the eastern U.S. It took many weeks to settle on a jury for John DeLorean's trial

THE TRIAL BEGINS

in California. We started soon after nine o'clock, and the jury of nine women and three men was impaneled by eleven-thirty.

They seated the ninety-six prospective jurors in the spectators' rows at first, and then as the judge asked each qualifying (or "voir dire") question, candidates were excused as they raised their hands to queries such as "Have you already formed an opinion in this case?" Those remaining were seated in the jury-box, twelve at a time, while the judge asked additional questions and listened to their concerns or answered their questions.

Some of them further disqualified themselves for various personal reasons or were excused for reasons such as health, work, hardship, and the like.

Meanwhile, each side had twenty preemptory challenges which could be used to excuse a juror for no stated reason, and this is where Donna Siers' expertise came into play. We listened for any revealing clues during their conversations with the judge, while at the same time following a master list of all prospective jurors which showed names, ages, and occupations.

Based partly on the results of our mock trial, our defense team wanted a jury of a certain age group, predominantly female, because women tend to be more sympathetic. They wanted fewer males, and they tried to avoid accidentally getting veterans of military service who might prejudge and not consider the evidence.

They wanted jurors whose professions dealt with people, like nurses, teachers, and personnel clerks, because people-oriented persons were more flexible and open-minded than those who dealt in inanimate or mechanical crafts.

Of our twenty allotted challenges each, we dismissed eighteen jurors and the prosecution dismissed seventeen. It all happened rather quickly, and the jury of twelve, plus two alternates, was then sworn and given their instructions by Judge Williams.

Opening statements began after a lunch recess, and the prosecution laid out its case in just twenty minutes, which frankly surprised me. I was expecting its opening remarks to be much longer. My first reaction was, "Is that all?"

I felt this way because the witness list they'd given us in pretrial hearings was so extensive, twenty-seven names, that I thought maybe they'd developed some new scenarios and loaded the list with witnesses who were prerehearsed.

It's a one-sided business to go up against the government in a CIPA-governed trial. The Classified Information Procedures Act provides that their side determines what information was or wasn't protected. So in addition to giving them a list of all the evidence we would present, we had to give them our witness list, plus we had to tell them just what each witness would probably say in both direct and cross-examination. It sounded to me like the fox guarding the hen house!

On the other hand, even though they were obligated under Rule 16, the Evidentiary Discovery Rule, to likewise give us a list of witnesses and evidence they would put on, they were under no obligation to tell us anything about what their witnesses would say.

For example, they brought in a witness from South Africa who, at their request, had taken color photos of locations in Tokyo pertinent to my story. Two florists were flown in from San Francisco to identify an FBI agent who had sent flowers to the San Francisco Soviet Consulate. Apparently he had enclosed a coded note to try to reenact my contact there.

As it turned out, we were unduly concerned about a flock of "mystery witnesses" that turned out to be inconsequential. No wonder their opening statement was comparatively short. It basically covered what actually happened—with two major differences.

First, they claimed my statements to the FBI were confessions, and they certainly were not. Second, because Richardson had warned me to "say nothing to the FBI," my statements to the FBI were somewhat contorted, narrative cover stories. All I could do back then was lay down a trail with gaping holes they'd have to check with the CIA because I was naively confident that the Agency would pull me out as soon as they knew of the situation.

In their opening statement and in the subsequent questioning of FBI witnesses, they tried to convince the jury that I was a shifty liar who was "caught" and had "confessed." During the trial, Brent challenged them to produce a single signed document resembling a confession, but they were unable to do so.

Now it was our turn. After the prosecution's opening statement, Brent got up and said, "Ladies and gentlemen of the jury. Under American law, the burden of proof that Richard Craig Smith is guilty lies with the prosecution. The defendant is innocent until guilt is proven beyond a reasonable doubt. He doesn't even have to testify. He doesn't have to say anything."

Brent continued. "But in this particular trial, we're going to do it differently. We're going to relieve the prosecution of that burden. We are going to assume that burden ourselves and prove to you that the defendant did not break the law."

This was superb showmanship on Brent's part because actually, the law on proof hadn't suddenly changed. But the way Brent tied this into his closing arguments on Friday clearly impressed the jury.

Now the parade of the government's witnesses began, twenty-two witnesses out of the twenty-seven on their original list. Some were:

1) Mike Waguespack, the FBI agent who arrested me at Dulles Airport
2) Mark Hoffman, Richardson's CIA assistant
3) Paul Shields, my former bishop and the FBI chief I telephoned
4) Rick Smith, my San Francisco FBI friend who investigated me
5) Pete Chase, the Salt Lake City FBI agent who interviewed Mavis Nelson
6) Ron Hilly, the first polygraph operator
7) John Murphy, the second polygraph operator
8) Paul Minor, the third polygraph operator
9) Noel Jones, my former boss in Army Intelligence

In every case, Joseph Aronica, the government's chief prosecutor, read questions from a typed script, and each agent responded with his memorized answer. The obvious problem was that after three to five minutes, each agent had to pull out his own copy and actually read his answers. Every time we'd object to these scripted interrogations, they'd put away their scripts, but in a few minutes out they would come again.

At one time, Aronica got distracted by something Brent said and appeared to totally lose his place, and since he'd been glued to his script, he seemed unable to get on track at all. He simply stopped the questioning and excused the witness.

Again and again, Aronica's master-script warped and twisted my words, taking them out of context in order to picture me as a deceptive liar who confessed when caught.

For example, the day after Rick Smith knocked on my door and flashed his FBI badge, he and I went across the street from the Hotel Utah to sit down and talk inside Temple Square. I said, "Rick, are you wearing a wire (hidden tape-recorder)?" Supposedly quoting, from his official agent report, Agent Smith, in his testimony described the conversation in terms of a confession and a request to make a "deal" for "immunity" when in fact I had never used either of those words with Rick Smith.

Again in Temple Square a moment later I said, "Rick, yesterday was the worst day of my life," But the script had him misquoting again, suggesting that my statement was an admission of guilt rather than a realization that the CIA backstopping that had been promised wasn't there!

Then a little later, I actually said, "Rick, this isn't what you think it is," meaning, of course, that I couldn't tell him that I was working for the Agency. It was written in the report, "Rick, I didn't do it for the reason you think I did it."

My statements to Rick were carefully altered, and in every case the FBI reports and the agents testimonies were rendered so as to cast the worst possible light and interpretation. It was part of the investigative mind set. Much of Rick's testimony was simply asking him to agree to other agents' testimony about the events of the investigation. Even Rick Smith, my friend, who really did an impartial job of investigating my story. It was a sad sight to see him look downward, avoid my eyes, and say, "Yes, that's pretty much the way it happened."

At one point, I had leaned over to Brent and said, "Rick Smith didn't write it that way!" When we quickly dug out the FBI report, Rick Smith had not used that wording. So when Brent cross-examined Rick, he asked him, "Did you really mean this?" and he got Rick to waffle a little. "As a matter of fact, didn't you say in your own report . . . ?" Brent stated the correct wording, and Rick said he wasn't sure.

"Well, let's get the report out and look at it." Brent opened the report, read the correct version, and Rick said yes, he guessed he did say it differently, after all.

Brent was a genius not only at getting at the truth, but showing the jury that scripted words were being placed in the mouths of otherwise honest FBI agents.

But that didn't take away from the facts that were true and damning. Even though my attorneys could rehabilitate each scripted distortion, the damage was piling up, especially because of the trail of cover stories I had told the FBI.

And so it went, all day Tuesday and half of Wednesday. Aronica would bury us with dirt, and we'd have to dig ourselves back out of the hole each time.

A few ridiculous things happened, however, that demonstrated to the jury how desperate the government was to get me put away.

First, they spent many thousand dollars on charts and other graphics with all kinds of elaborate and fancy three-dimensional artwork. It was pure flamboyance, graphic overkill, and when they began bringing it out and setting it up, Judge Williams was not particularly impressed.

Joseph Aronica explained that the government felt the jury needed a more detailed and graphic understanding of my misdeeds. The judge threw out about two-thirds of their elaborate visual aids and he did so on at least three different occasions during the trial, warning that the court room was not a graphic arts show and that the jury was surely competent to understand the evidence.

It was this attempt at overkill that inspired Brent and me to effectively use an old battered blackboard when he presented his closing arguments to the jury later on in the trial.

It was fascinating to contrast the subtle showmanship Brent was so good at with the heavy-handed approach by the prosecution.

Another waste of taxpayers' money occurred when the government flew Harriet Styler in from Salt Lake City. She was the trustee in both of my bankruptcies, company and personal. They tried to discredit me by claiming that I'd falsified my personal debt disclosure by omitting a company note on which I had a contingent liability. On cross-examination, it was established that my former attorney had prepared the papers and that the omission was reasonable under the circumstances.

One of the government's witnesses was actually canceled by Ken Melson, Aronica's assistant prosecutor. This witness was a parking meter official in Salt Lake City, but we didn't know that when we got the government's witness list with all the unknown names on it. The prosecution would only say that those names were "surprise witnesses," and "we don't have to tell you who they are."

We were allowed, however, to phone them and ask if they were willing to tell us what they would probably say. This parking meter official said he was being flown out to testify that meters in downtown Salt Lake City don't require coins after six o'clock in the evening. We found out the next day why this seemingly insignificant fact was so important. Ken Melson called Bill Cummings on April first. Ken said, "Bill, we're trying to cut costs at Judge Williams' request, so we'll not bring out this Salt Lake City official, if your side will stipulate that coins are not required in their meters after six o'clock."

Bill said, "Why?"

Melson was apparently too embarrassed to give Bill the reason at first, but he was trapped now. He said, "Well, when the defendant left the Hotel Utah for a few minutes saying he needed to check his meter, one of the FBI agents, Pete Chase, glanced at his watch and noted it was six-fifteen, and therefore the defendant had lied."

Bill was incredulous at first. Then, remembering what day it was, he said, "Ken, this is an April Fool's joke, isn't it?"

"No, it isn't."

Bill said, "You're kidding me! You mean to say that you're basing your whole case on this kind of testimony?"

"Will you so stipulate, so we can save bringing out this witness?"

Bill just said, "You bring him!" And he slammed down the phone.

This is the only time I ever saw Bill get angry. He was furious because it was ludicrous to rake up such imagined dirt. But it showed us how very little they really had in their case, and later in the trial some of their courtroom antics telegraphed this message to the jury, too.

The government's case was undermined by two glaring mistakes the prosecution made. The first was in overestimating the ability of FBI agents to memorize a script and make it sound natural and sincere. So Joseph Aronica found himself caught between two impossible positions. Either he had his people reading their pat answers to his questions or they got lost trying to ad-lib their dialogue, especially in cross-examination by our attorneys. The jury seemed to see through this. Secondly, they saw the government reaching for straws with a bizarre collection of far-fetched witnesses like Harriet Styler and the florists from San Francisco. The government's case lost credibility both ways.

Just before the lunch break on Wednesday, the prosecution finished examining the rest of their twenty-two witnesses, including several technical and background people. And after the equivalent of two full days of testimony, some terribly damaging and some flamboyant overkill, the government rested its case about a half-day early.

This presented a real problem for us because we had scheduled our out-of-town witnesses to arrive Wednesday evening and testify Thursday. Now we had a long afternoon with only our character witnesses: my father, Fred Schwendiman, my brothers Hy and Todd, and a few more similarly bland witnesses.

There was no way that I could go on myself until the very end, with Sherry and Susan testifying just before me.

We would have given anything to be able to persuade Judge Williams to adjourn for the day on that Wednesday noon, but he had already announced that we'd go every day from nine until six and finish this entire case, including jury deliberations, that weekend—including Saturday and Sunday if necessary.

So following the government's two days of muck-raking, we had to put on a passive parade of conservative, law-abiding citizens who could tell the jury nothing about the details of the case itself.

All they could do was tell them what a nice guy I was.

It was a long afternoon, and we felt like it ended in disaster.

18

Our Defense Bogs Down

All week long the press had been crowding us for news of a breakthrough in our defense, and we'd been assuring them that we did have strong evidence that we were ready to present to the jury.

Their reaction to the procession of family and intimate friends telling the court how sweet a child and how kind a father and husband I'd been was one of total incredulity after hearing the government's biting accusations.

Media people swarmed around our attorneys and asked, "Is this all you've got?"

Charles Sherrill, a correspondent for KSL, the Salt Lake CBS affiliate, said, "I thought we were going to hear some really powerful stuff. If that's all you've got, you're dead!"

The prosecution killed us that day, and we really felt badly. Looking backward later, perhaps that made us all the more determined that evening to prepare for the big day on Thursday when all our superstars would testify. It was expected that I would be on the stand for several hours.

Donna Siers continued her job of coaching and preparing witnesses that evening while Brent and I worked to prepare for my single appearance on Thursday. Meanwhile, Bill Cummings worked with Susan, preparing her to testify. We all knew that this was going to be our only chance to persuade the jury of the propriety and the rightness of our defense. The diligence of our team members was an inspiration to everyone.

One heavy, dark cloud hung over us, though. We couldn't use one single page of the hundreds of pages of evidence we'd accumulated pertaining to Bishop-Baldwin. About four hundred of these documents contained some direct reference to the CIA and clearly linked CMI Investment Co., Bishop-Baldwin, Richardson/Cavannaugh, and my contact-phone number—all to the Agency. Copies of these documents had been presented in pretrial hearings and now sat in Judge Richard Williams' chambers, sealed by an order of the Fourth Circuit Court. They could easily have tipped the scales with the jury and kept me from spending the rest of my life in prison, but the government had succeeded in getting them quashed entirely.

This was the atmosphere in which my attorneys and I worked on into the night, sharpening our final attempt to win my freedom when court reconvened the next morning.

There were just seven witnesses left for Bill and Brent to put on the stand that final day.

Dr. Sherry Skidmore would use an overhead projector to present the highlights of her twenty-page evaluation, testifying that the results of her testing clearly suggested I was telling the truth and, in fact, had been so programmed throughout my life that I would be almost incapable of betraying my country.

Mavis Nelson, my former secretary during the Timespan years when I was actually in frequent touch with Ken White, would testify she had strict orders that whenever Ken White called and asked for me, she was to interrupt any meeting or other business to put me on the phone with him. She would describe White's voice and manner on the phone and help him come alive for the jury.

She would also testify that when Pete Chase, the Salt Lake City FBI agent, interviewed her some time after I had closed the Timespan office and moved away, Chase had basically admitted that the FBI knew I had been working for the CIA. She would identify the notarized transcript of that conversation that we'd been saving for two-and-a-half years, and confirm that she had made that transcript the day after her conversation with Chase.

Next, we had brought the former telephone receptionist for Bishop-Baldwin over from Honolulu. She would testify that hers was the voice that answered Craig Smith's many calls to the contact-phone number which was one of Bishop Baldwin's private numbers. She would confirm that Craig Smith always asked for Ken White and only Ken White, and that she would write a phone message memo for Ken White, requesting that he return Craig Smith's call. She would say that she knew that Bishop Baldwin and CMI Investment Co. both had something to do with the Central Intelligence Agency, but she didn't know what the exact connection was.

Ron Rewald was already in town, having been transferred from the federal penitentiary at Terminal Island near Los Angeles and held at my old alma mater, the Fairfax County jail.

He would go on the stand next and explain the connection between Bishop-Baldwin and the CIA, having maintained ever since his arrest that he also was a CIA agent. As a former principal of Bishop-Baldwin, he'd be better qualified than anyone else to explain how CMI Investment Co. was a subsidiary company on paper, (sometimes called a "notional" company by legal experts) set up by Charles L. Richardson/Richard P. Cavannaugh. It had been for the purpose of managing the activities of CIA agents under his direction throughout the Pacific Rim. Rewald would explain how funding was accomplished and contact maintained. It was obvious to all of us that, outside of my testimony, Ron Rewald would be our second most important witness.

I say second most important because Charles L. Richardson/ Richard P. Cavannaugh could possibly be our most important witness. Right up until Thursday morning, none of us knew just how to play the "Richardson card."

Two years earlier we had learned from Ron Rewald the identity and involvement of Charles L. Richardson in the CIA and in Bishop-Baldwin. We began licking our chops to get him on the witness stand, show him our Bishop-Baldwin-CIA documents, and force him to verify my story.

But now there were no documents, no proof, no hard evidence, and we feared we might get nothing but a stonewall from him, which in the eyes of the jury, could actually support the government's own case. In a worst-case scenario, he could destroy us. It was a very real fear, and Bill Cummings was especially concerned that we reconsider our plan to call him as a witness.

However, Brent Carruth didn't fear anyone or anything, and we were anxious to face Richardson in court for personal reasons. I wanted the opportunity to prove to the world that it was a network of Charles L. Richardson's (and the Agency's) lies, greed, and corruption that got me into trouble with the FBI in the first place.

Even more important, their blunders and misconduct cost our nation a vital important opportunity to penetrate the Soviet KGB. The possibility exists that these mistakes cost us the opportunity of slowing down the avalanche of real spies like Walker and Whitworth by exposing their contacts before the damage began.

There are possibly disloyal Americans in the early stages right now of being lured by the Soviets to sell their country's secrets for cash.

How many tragic information hemorrhages will we discover five, ten, twenty years from now that could have been prevented by our getting further inside the KGB before they happen?

That's what fueled the fire in me. I wanted to get Richardson on the stand and expose him for what he was and for what he did. For that reason the original decision to get Richardson for a witness became an important goal. We had only one problem; we didn't know where he was. When the Honolulu operation folded, he took "early retirement" and disappeared. We found out later he was comfortably secure in an expensive home near Camelback Mountain, outside of Phoenix, Arizona.

For two years we'd tried to get the government to subpoena him, but the government had said, "He doesn't work for us anymore, and we don't have any obligation to produce him."

Gradually we gave up hope of finding him and decided to build our case around the government's refusal to put him on the stand. We would then show the jury how afraid of Richardson's testimony the government was.

The whole picture changed when we lost our precious trunkload of evidence to the Fourth Circuit Court. Now we needed two things. First, we needed Richardson. Second, we needed some way to get him to substitute himself for our suppressed evidence. Both bordered on the impossible.

We needed a couple of miracles!

During the last weeks before the trial began, we pressed hard for Richardson, but the prosecution thwarted us on every move. As late as the Friday morning before the trial, they still said, "We don't know where he is."

By then the time was so short, we played a long shot. We went to Judge Williams and told him that if he would order them to give us Richarson's address and phone number, we would serve a subpoena ourselves. The judge agreed, approved our subpoena, and gave the prosecution until the end of the day to give us the information we needed to serve it. They did not comply.

On the Sunday evening before the trial, we were in Bill's office involved in last minute preparations when a small envelope was slipped under the door and a messenger left without our seeing him. It was Richardson's address and telephone number in Phoenix!

We rushed over to our apartment, dialed the number, and waited. There was no answer!

Then Brent got on the phone to Ken Melson, Aronica's assistant and said, "Ken, how come we didn't get this information until tonight? Don't you think this is a little ridiculous? We were supposed to have this by the close of business on Friday. Here it is Sunday night. We've just called this number and there's nobody there."

Ken said, "Well that's funny because we just talked to him last night." That meant that they had known his phone number the day before.

Brent said, "If you just talked to him last night, it's no wonder we don't get an answer tonight. Where'd you tell him to go?"

We suspected they had called him, perhaps on Saturday, and informed them that they had to give us the phone number, and they were going to do it tomorrow, so don't answer the phone. He would need to be out of there so he couldn't be served with a subpoena.

We also felt that the government's whole objective was to keep Richardson out of our reach, but Ken Melson had slipped when he admitted talking to him the day before. That's witness tampering, and we could have gone in the next day and had the judge declare a mistrial.

Brent continued, with Melson on the other end of the phone. "That's wonderful! I'm really happy you've told us that you talked to our witness on the telephone. We'll just have to see what Judge Williams has to say about this tomorrow!" Brent hung up the phone.

In a short while, Melson called back and said, "We'll have Richardson there."

I'm convinced that Ken Melson's slip of the tongue was the only way we could have gotten Charles L. Richardson on the witness stand.

Monday morning, during jury selection, Brent got a message to call Charles L. Richardson in Phoenix, so Brent went to Bill's office at the noon break and called him. At last, Brent was hearing Richardson's voice for the first time.

Richardson said, "Well, I guess it's about time that you and I met. I've been hearing a lot about you. I think it's about time we had it out, so I'm going to come out and bury you!"

The arrogant voice on the phone threatening to bury Brent Carruth was a red-flag challenge. That was all Brent needed—he would tear him apart!

OUR DEFENSE BOGS DOWN

Bill Cummings became more than a little nervous, not because he was easily intimidated, but because we'd built our defense around Richardson's absence, and now he would be there.

Ron Rewald panicked. Rewald told us that Richardson was the most intelligent, the most conniving, the most shrewd, ruthless, and dangerous person he'd ever met; and that he'd lie, he'd cheat, he'd do anything to hurt us. He said that even if he showed up, we'd be crazy to call him to testify. "He'll eat you for lunch!" Rewald was almost afraid to testify himself, if Richardson came to the courtroom.

Charles L. Richardson/Richard P. Cavannaugh did indeed come to the U.S. District Court in Alexandria on Thursday, but at six o'clock Wednesday evening, after the court adjourned, my attorneys and I were privately summoned to the judge's chambers. Judge Williams told us that after we had finessed the prosecution and they agreed to produce Richardson, they immediately went up to the Fourth Circuit again. The persuaded one of the judges to write an interpretation of the court's en banc CIPA ruling to the effect that if all the sealed documents were inadmissible, then anything that Richardson would say pertaining to those documents was, by extension, also inadmissible. We wouldn't be able to ask questions in any area so covered. Those were the very areas we really needed to question him on. One of our attorneys said, "That's not fair!"

Judge Williams answered that his hands were tied. If he didn't follow this new interpretation, we could wind up with a mistrial.

On the way back to Bill's office, I dropped back a few steps, thinking to myself, how many times am I supposed to take this battering by the very government I love with all my heart? I didn't know how much more my body and soul could stand.

We soon arrived at Bill's office and worked on witness preparation. We held a late night strategy meeting, but it was too late to devise an entirely new game plan.

I left the office at eleven-thirty, utterly frustrated. Never before had I felt so crushed, dejected, and almost defeated.

19

Our Defense Is Resurrected

Early on Thursday morning, April 10th 1986, I met Brent Carruth at Bill Cummings' office. He had a big smile on his face and said, "I haven't slept all night, but I think everything's under control."

He'd stayed up all night working out a new plan and then called the court clerk very early in the morning and convinced her to call the judge and arrange a phone conversation with him.

Brent told the judge in essence, that since the Fourth Circuit Court's ruling virtually precluded us from asking Mr. Richardson the very questions that were relevant to our case, and since there is certain information concerning Mr. Richardson and his affiliation with the CIA that we believed to be important for the jury to know, Brent suggested that it might not be inappropriate for the court itself to ask certain questions that might open the door, depending on Mr. Richardson's answers, to cross-examination by either the defense or the prosecution.

He continued, suggesting that Judge Williams might call this witness and ask questions that were appropriate to the jury's consideration of the case itself, but which would not violate the Fourth Circuit's ruling. The judge agreed to consider the proposal.

Brent went even further in suggesting some possible questions which could be related to a selected group of documents that the judge was already familiar with, and which would easily show, by Richardson's answers whether he was answering truthfully or not. The judge again listened to Brent's suggested questions.

Finally Brent asked the judge if he would be willing to inform the jury if Richardson's testimony departed from the truth, and if, in the process of establishing the truth of matters at issue, we would be allowed to cross-examine the witness concerning that which came out of testimony discovered by the court itself. Again, Judge Williams agreed to consider the proposal.

This was a turning point in our seemingly hopeless defense. However, unless and until Richardson himself should open the door by being less than truthful, we still had absolutely no tangible, physical, documentary evidence that we could introduce—zero. But if the documents Brent sent along with the questions were, in fact, linked to Richardson's answers, they might then be admitted as part of the cross-examination.

I entered the courtroom feeling much encouraged. Brent had given us a new hope for the moment.

The morning's witnesses went well, and our case began to gather momentum. Sherry Skidmore was superb, and Mavis Nelson was courteous and professional. The prosecution insisted on asking her, in cross-examination, if it weren't true that she and I had had a love affair going on between us. Mavis assured the jury that had never been the case. Donna Siers told me later that the nine women on the jury were offended by such an unsavory and unwarranted allegation and were somewhat drawn to by defense by this tactic.

Next it was Ron Rewald's turn, and Assistant U.S. Attorney Ken Melson's cross-examination was so accusative and abrasive that the judge, on more than one occasion, warned him that his line and method of questioning was improper and not in accordance with the Federal procedure. Rewald responded well and was more than believable to the jury.

At last it was time to call Richardson into the courtroom. The prosecution was quite comfortable about this situation because they were sure that, because of the Fourth Circuit ruling, we would only be able to ask questions that Richardson could easily stonewall. If we couldn't produce any evidence to contradict his lies, Richardson could get away with them and make us look guilty of fabricating a flimsy scenario around Ron Rewald's story about the CIA-Bishop, Baldwin connection.

Joe Aronica seemed to be in the driver's seat. He'd win on Richardson's testimony either way, whether we questioned him or not.

Charles Richardson was brought into the courtroom and he walked confidently to the stand. Dressed in a sleekly tailored power suit, he was handsome, suave, self-assured, with a slick look of contempt for the whole process. This was the all-powerful Richardson/Cavanaugh that had been a mystery to us until now.

Judge Williams paused for a moment and then spoke, telling the jury that while the defense had in fact subpoenaed Mr. Richardson to the trial, the defense had chosen at this time not to call him as a witness.

Aronica almost smiled because it looked as though we'd lost our courage and would not risk putting him on the stand.

The judge then continued, adding that the prosecution had also chosen not to call Mr. Richardson.

The attorneys at the prosecutor's table were confident of our fear of Richardson and sat back to relax in the smug security of their position.

Then, over the objection of Mr. Aronica, Judge Williams then told the jury that he, the judge, was calling Richardson as a witness because neither side had chosen to do so, adding, "I am calling him now, because I don't know of anything that you plan to put on in rebuttal. I am calling him now, because I want the evidence in the record.

"And I don't want any parties to feel in any way obligated to call him, but I think the jury needs him to answer some questions."

Mr. Aronica again protested, now claiming that the government had intentions of calling Richardson as a rebuttal witness.

But Judge Williams, to make the situation clear to the jury, replied,

"But here again, so you don't mislead anybody, he came in here because the defendant asked to have him subpoenaed, and I ordered him brought here. Administer the oath."

After Richardson was sworn, the judge began.

Q   Please state your name for the record.
A   Charles Richardson.
Q   And where do you live, Mr. Richardson?
A   I am a California resident; I live in California and part time in Arizona.
Q   Are you presently employed?
A   I am an independent contractor.
Q   There has been testimony that you previously lived in Honolulu, Hawaii, and were connected with the CIA while you lived in Honolulu; is that correct?
A   I have never lived in Honolulu; I have visited there.
Q   All right. Were you connected with the CIA in Honolulu?
A   I have visited there while connected with the CIA, yes.

The questioning went on, with Judge Williams careful to stay within the guidelines established by the Fourth Circuit.

Q   Did you have a C.M.I. business card with your name on it?
A   Yes I did. That was for use in other areas.
Q   And that the telephone number for C.M.I. rang in and at a facility called Bishop-Baldwin; is that correct?
A   That is correct.
Q   And did you have an arrangement whereby calls that came in to certain people at that number were relayed on to you?
A   No; there was no such arrangement.

The testimony was in direct contrast to that of Trish Gallo and Ronald Rewald. Further questioning by Judge Williams revealed that Richardson had requested retirement because his superiors at the CIA were, in his words, "definitely unhappy" with his financial dealings in Bishop-Baldwin.

The judge than released Richardson, indicating that if the prosecution wanted to call him as a witness in rebuttal to the information that the jury had heard, they could do so, but that the defense would then have an opportunity to re-cross the witness, opening the door for even more damaging information to come out. He then said to the jury, "That is the court's evidence. Ladies and gentlemen, let me give you another status report, the defendant has concluded the evidence that he is going to put on and I have plugged in the evidence that the court felt that you ought to have. And now the government, if it is advised to do so, may put on rebuttal evidence."

Two very important things were happening at this point. Not only had the judge permitted the jury to understand the reality of Richardson's tie to the CIA, but the prosecutors were becoming increasing agitated. They might make the mistake of trying to repair the damage the only way they knew how—by questioning Richardson further in an effort to rehabilitate his testimony. This was exactly what my attorneys wanted because it would allow us to cross-examine the witness even further and possibly get some of the government's classified documents into evidence.

Brent had made a momentous decision in not accepting the judge's offer to call the witness for the defense, but he had gambled on Mr. Aronica's concern about the impression Richardson's testimony had on the jury and that he would call him, allowing Brent the last word. If Aronica refused, however, the door was closed.

Aronica rose and asked that Richardson be recalled. As he did so, Judge Williams admonished him that if there was any inconsistency in the testimony that he gives as a prosecution witness (inconsistent with the documents that had been provided), he would make a motion to allow the defense to use that information as part of our case.

Mr. Aronica questioned:

Q   I want to draw your attention to June, 1983. Did you have occasion to talk to a person who identified himself as Richard Craig Smith?

A   Yes, I did; on the telephone.

It was impossible to deny the telephone conversation because in discovery the government had produced a letter identifying Richardson as the person who had spoken with me after I had set up the call through Paul Shields. He had to say yes.

Q And what was that conversation?

A I don't recall precisely, but I had been called by the FBI, given minimal information and an introduction telephone where I could reach him, and had been told that he felt he had information that might be of use or interest to the agency.

Q And did you call him back?

Richardson replied that he had in fact returned the call, but in response to Mr. Aronica's question whether he had told me to keep quiet about my activities in Tokyo, of course, he responded that he had never so advised me. Before sitting down, because he knew Brent would raise the issue, Aronica asked Mr. Richardson about his retirement which turned out to be not merely voluntary, but as Aronica had to explain to the jury, because of the difficulty Richardson had had with the CIA, the voluntary termination was in reality involuntary.

Brent then stood to cross-examine the witness.

Q Isn't it a fact, Mr. Richardson, that C.M.I. was a cover location that was arranged for you at Bishop-Baldwin; isn't that a fact?

It was a cover arrangement that was arranged by Mr. Rewald.

Mr. Aronica objected to the question, but Judge Williams responded, "I asked that same question, and he gave a slightly different answer; but your objection is overruled. I will permit his answer to stand."

Brent continued:

Q Isn't it a fact, sir, that on or around April and May of 1983, that you told intentional falsehoods to the Central Intelligence Agency headquarters here in Washington concerning your relationship with Bishop-Baldwin?

Richardson was forced to admit that he had mislead his own headquarters. In his words, he had "omitted certain information" about his dealings with Bishop-Baldwin, suggesting that the indiscretions had had only to do with his investments there, but the evidence suggested otherwise.

The key elements of our defense, even though we were not permitted to place the classified evidence before the jury had been established; the link between the CIA and Bishop-Baldwin, the telephone number that had rung in Honolulu, the CIA's difficulty and withdrawal from Bishop-Baldwin just as my communication with White and Ishida had dried up, and a CIA agent who had admitted talking to me on the day I had called to recontact the agency and his admissions that he had lied even to his own superiors.

Aronica could do nothing on recross, so the witness was excused, and a significant part of the government's case went into the ashcan.

We still had two witnesses left, Susan and me.

Bill put Susan on the stand. He asked her about our life together and about how I behaved when I was operational compared to when I was not working. He asked about the Honolulu trip—did I go to a meeting? Did I seem different afterward? He asked about her faith and belief in me and about my loyalty to the United States.

Susan said, "There's no person on this earth who loves his country more than Craig!" Susan finished in about half an hour, and several of the women jurors were weeping.

Brent whispered in my ear, "If we win, you can give Susan all the credit."

It was my turn, at last, to tell my story to the jury.

For a moment, before I was called to the stand, I reflected on the blessing Fred Schwendiman had given me the night before. In the blessing he had said, "You will be calm. You will be clear of thought, and you will be able to recall the information that will be important to your testimony." I was calm—the Richardson fireworks had paved the way for me to be credible and open.

However, something else happened the night before, just after I received that blessing from Fred. As Brent and I began our preparation for my appearance, I had a very strong impression that, after asking my name, Brent's very first question should be, "Are you a spy?"

I would answer, "Yes."

This would defuse immediately the spy issue and get the jury thinking positively instead of negatively.

Brent had agreed.

Now I was on the witness stand itself. The first question came as planned and I answered yes.

Brent then asked, "What country did you spy for?"

"The United States of America." The effect was electric.

Brent asked dozens of questions which led the interview through my entire story in about an hour and a half. But he didn't once simply turn me loose to "tell us in your own words. . . ." Instead, Brent maintained control at all times as we had rehearsed. I answered yes or no or explained my answer in twenty-five words or less.

The testimony went well, thanks to Donna Siers, who had coached me to prepare mentally by assembling the real facts. I was able to stay with the truth in direct and cross-examination.

After the basic story, Brent needed to counter some of the FBI testimony. "Why did you tell devious stories to the FBI?"

I answered, "Because I'd been given strict orders not to tell any of the facts about the CIA."

"By whom?"

"By the CIA in San Francisco" I replied.

Richardson had already admitted that he had talked to me on the telephone in June of 1983, but he denied that he told me to keep quiet. The jury would have to weigh his story against mine, and I was sure I would win.

Brent also asked, "When was the first time you told me you'd been working for the CIA?"

"In a church basement in McLean, Virginia, on May 12, 1984."

"What was my response?"

I replied, "You said I was crazy."

Finally, to bring my story to a close, Brent asked, "What government agency were you working for?"

"The Central Intelligence Agency of the United States of America."

He then asked, "Did you ever, at any time, give to the KGB, or to anyone else, any information that wasn't authorized?"

"No."

"Did you do anything other than follow CIA orders?"

"No, except to try and contact my case officer, and that wasn't illegal or disloyal—just stupid."

Brent asked two final questions. "Are you loyal to the United States of America?"

"Absolutely."

"Would you do this again, if called?"

"Yes."

On cross-examination, Joseph Aronica asked relatively few questions, primarily trying to get me to say that I had "confessed" to the FBI agents.

I said that I had never at any time confessed.

The only issue they had left was to produce a delinquent American Express bill for $3,800, left over from my last few months' working as a civilian in the Army. I had paid it off over the next few months out of my Timespan salary.

The prosecution tried to claim that this debt was my motivation for deciding to sell secrets to the Soviets. But I had paid it off in early 1980 and made my first contact with the KGB in November of 1982, two-and-a-half years later. Brent brought this out in two simple questions during recross-examination, and the defense rested its case.

When I came down off the stand after two-and-a-half hours, Brent and Bill both said that they never would have believed that I could have remained so calm. They said that between Susan and me, the jury couldn't fail to believe us.

OUR DEFENSE IS RESURRECTED

The court was then adjourned, to reconvene the next morning for closing arguments.

We were next faced with the decision of which of our attorneys would give the closing statement summing up our case. Donna Siers and Sherry Skidmore thought it should be Bill Cummings, not only because this was his home turf and his courtroom, but because of his warmth and polite manner which would have a positive effect on the nine women of the jury. I leaned in that direction, too, feeling that Bill's demeanor would allow anyone Brent might have alienated to save face and accept Bill's arguments.

Brent and I talked about it after adjournment that day and Brent said, "Craig, it's your decision and yours alone. Only one of us can give the close, and we'll both agree with your decision and help the other."

Then he went on to say, "Remember, when this is over, Bill and I are going home, but you'll either go home or go to prison. So you decide."

That evening at the apartment the family gathered to offer prayer. Afterward, there was no doubt as to who would present the closing argument the following day. Every member of the family agreed, to a person, that it would be Brent Carruth.

I didn't have the stamina left that night to tell Bill, so Hy offered to call him and explain that the family wanted the member of our own faith to close. Bill understood and supported the decision.

Now it was up to me to help Brent prepare, and that took half the night. Two questions kept surfacing in my thoughts. What would tomorrow bring? Had we made the right choice?

20

Closing Arguments

Joseph Aronica spoke first, Friday morning, April 11th, 1986, to sum up the prosecution's case. He read his entire closing argument from a typed script. Aronica methodically took us through the highlights of the FBI testimony, once more using his elaborate charts, pictures, photo-collages, ribbons, arrows, graphs—you name it.

The prosecution's closing statement was very slick in its preparation and smoothly read by Mr. Aronica. It contained nothing new and, surprisingly, nothing inflammatory. But it was logical, and what was most discouraging, it sounded reasonable and plausible.

The case against Richard Craig Smith was simple. He did it and admits he did it. He got caught and confessed. The prosecution rests.

I said there was nothing inflammatory. True. That really bothered me because unless I misread Aronica's personality, he thrived on intimidating. He would have his chance for that later because the prosecution got one more inning after the defense presented its close. Perhaps I was still going to get cremated by Aronica.

* * * * *

We had been inspired by Aronica's graphic overkill to go out and find an old, ragged blackboard to use in our final arguments. We found one, and Brent and I spent hours the night before, working out the staging and the other details.

We wanted the blackboard so Brent could conduct an old-fashioned schoolhouse session of reading, writing and arithmetic. We knew that each day the jurors were given pencils and spiral steno-books for notes. When Brent would enumerate on the blackboard, we wanted all heads to go down and all pencils to write with him, recording his notes from the blackboard.

It actually worked. When Brent got up and addressed the jury, he presented a different contrast to Joseph Aronica. Brent never read and almost never used notes. He just talked from the heart and ad-libbed his way through.

He said to the jury, "On the first day of the trial, I told you that we would accept the burden of proving Richard Craig Smith is not guilty of the charges.

"I told you there would be no signed confessions presented. There haven't been.

"I told you we'd show that the CIA had been involved with Bishop-Baldwin. They have been.

"I told you that Craig had a phone number that we have traced to the CIA. We've shown you that.

"Now here's the reality. What this case is really all about is that in the spring of 1983, the CIA, out of control in Honolulu, pulled the plug, and Craig Smith got left out in the cold. The government now has come after him and told you all the things that he did.

"They've charged him with two counts of espionage, one count of conspiracy, and two counts of selling U.S. secrets to the Soviets.

"If he's done these things, in order to convict him, the law says the burden of proof is on the government. But they haven't proven a thing.

"Now what I'm going to do, since we, the defense, assumed the burden of proof that he is innocent, is to list the issues the government has failed to respond to. Now write these down with me."

Brent took a fat piece of chalk and wrote on the board as he ticked off each item. Sure enough, they wrote right along with him.

"1. They have not denied that the CIA was tied in with Bishop-Baldwin.

"2. They have not denied that Charles Richardson talked to Craig Smith.

"3. They have not denied that Craig Smith had a Honolulu CIA phone number.

"4. They have not denied that Craig Smith called that number and left messages for a CIA agent named Ken White.

"5. They have not denied that CIA agent Ken White called Craig Smith's office in Salt Lake City and talked to Craig and his secretary, Mavis Nelson.

"6. They have not denied that Craig Smith authenticated CIA contacts with Charles L. Richardson's other name and title: Richard P. Cavannaugh, President of CMI Investment Co.

"7. They have not denied that Pete Chase, Salt Lake City FBI agent, told Mavis Nelson that the FBI knew Craig Smith was working for the CIA.

"8. They have not denied that Charles L. Richardson has lied repeatedly about all the above and more."

It went on for a total of fifteen points on the blackboard. He'd write and they'd write.

Brent rolled on telling them, in essence, "Now we've proven that these are the facts, and they haven't denied it. Unless they either deny or in some way explain these facts that we've already proven, they must be true.

"The reality here is that the government has not proven their case. On the contrary, we have proven our case.

"Now the government has one more chance to make their case. But we don't have another chance. You have to accept what we're telling you right now because this is it. This is the last chance we get.

"So the government gets one more chance, and I've made it easy for them because I've given them a list of things that they need to answer. And if they can answer them, you have an obligation to convict Richard Craig Smith on all five counts."

Then Brent turned to Aronica and said, "I challenge you to answer any one of these!"

He then turned back to the jury and said, "The government will not only fail to answer all of them—they'll not be able to answer a single one of them. And if they fail to answer a single one of them, then your duty is to find this man 'not guilty!' "

Then Brent sat down.

After a short recess, Aronica began his rebuttal. For the next forty minutes, he went into a tirade. He spewed out vituperations and made every conceivable effort to incite emotions. He pounded on the table and beat on the podium.

"In an attempt to escape, to suggest that the CIA would have someone working as a double agent for them, and another arm of the government bringing him into the court and prosecuting him is preposterous. It's preposterous! Your government, our government doesn't work that way."

Through all his tirade, he didn't address one single item listed on the blackboard, and the jurors had their pencils poised to capture any single rebuttal to our fifteen points.

There were none because Aronica didn't have any.

Yet he displayed such hatred, anger and vitriolic language about me that, frankly, it scared me. To have anyone talk about me with such venom in his heart was terrifying.

Real panic was beginning to grip me. I tried to hide it because I didn't want to show Susan any negative feelings. But Joseph Aronica had truly gotten to me, and for the first time in this entire crisis—for the first time in three long years—I imagined myself going out the door in handcuffs, back to the hell of prison.

21

My Faith Is Tested

I found myself moving out of the courtroom for another recess, but I was in a kind of fog. I sat down somewhere out of the way and rested my forehead on my hands. My ears were still ringing, my throat was dry, and my eyes were filling with tears. I have to confess that at this point I was lower than low. I was down.

I must confess further that I'd been a little disappointed with Brent's low-profile, logical closing argument. I didn't think it had been very effective. Later on I learned just how effective it really had been. But from the moment Brent had finished and during the recess before Aronica's rebuttal, I was really concerned.

Sherry had reported to me privately, when we were discussing who would give the close, that Brent had said something on the way back from the courthouse Wednesday evening. It happened after the disaster of the first day we began our defense. Apparently Brent had made the comment, "I think he's going down!"

When I'd heard that Brent himself had admitted a crisis of confidence, I was troubled. Had I made a mistake in selecting Brent over Bill?

After Joseph Aronica had worked me over for forty interminable minutes, all I could think of was why hadn't Brent given me a chance to fight against this cancer? Why couldn't I have shown my true patriotism by giving an emotional antidote to the bashing I had been forced to take? I was reasonably articulate. I could communicate my deepest feelings of patriotism to a jury. Why wasn't I asked how I felt about having risked my life for my country—placing myself in the hands of the enemy—only to be senselessly pilloried by this federal prosecutor?

* * * * *

Time stood still as I thought of all the "if onlys" in my life. If only I'd dropped the case instead of phoning Paul Shields that morning in San Francisco. If only I'd told the FBI the full story at the outset instead of trying to protect what had turned out to be a rogue CIA operation. If only I'd had better luck with my business. If only I'd finished college. If only I'd been a better husband and father all these years.

A silent prayer rose in my heart as I questioned why this was happening to me. Then I thought of Christ in Gethsemane. There never was a more perfect man, yet he was about to be crucified. He said, "Father, if it be possible let this cup pass from me: nevertheless, not as I will, but as thou wilt." I thought of Jesus. I thought of His mere thirty-three years of life and the fact that he never hated his oppressors. In fact, he loved all mankind.

He said, "Forgive them, Father, for they know not what they do." Could I love my enemies to that perfect degree?

Right then, as I faced forty years in prison, I looked back and saw the gaps where I should have worked harder, or been smarter, or had fewer faults, or been more successful.

* * * * *

Suddenly I felt Susan's hand on my cheek. She was saying, "Did you fall asleep?"

It was the sweetest sound in the whole world. I had drifted off and dreamed the patchwork of thoughts recounted here. In essence, my faith was being tested. But I had met and passed that test before, and I could pass it again.

I stood up, gave Susan a hug, and went back into the courtroom, determined to keep my courage up and my confidence high, no matter what happened.

22

The Verdict

When we came back into the courtroom, the judge gave his instructions to the jury, which took about forty-five minutes. Their final instructions, were to select a foreman, go to lunch, and return to begin deliberations as soon as possible.

As we started out of the courtroom, Brent said, "I think we'll have an acquittal, but it will take about four days of deliberations to get there." Then he added, "It has to take at least two days, or it could go badly for Craig."

Once the trial was over and the jury began their deliberations, I had to stay in the building until the jury went home for the night. No one can guess just when a verdict might be reached, and the court must be able to hear the verdict almost immediately. That's why the marshals see to it that the defendant remains in the building, along with the judge and at least one attorney from each side.

We went out for lunch and then returned to the witness room. Even though the family and all the witnesses and members of our defense team were there, I was really down.

We joined in prayer again, and Fred Schwendiman led us. We prayed that the jury would be given guidance and inspiration to evaluate the truthfulness of the statements given to them. We prayed that they would be guided to do what was right.

Then we sat down and waited. Everyone was still there, but the atmosphere was dark—almost like a funeral. Nobody knew what to say to each other, so people would try to make small talk. We'd look for little things to distract ourselves from the slow passage of time.

By mid-afternoon it began to lighten up a little bit, as we got the courage to laugh a little and try to feel like our natural selves. Things became more relaxed and informal.

By four-thirty or five o'clock, people started drifting off because if looked like we would be there again tomorrow, and maybe longer. Eventually, only Susan and I who remained, and that's when it really got to be heavy. I found myself thinking that at some point in time—and that time had now come—we would have to face the "What ifs. . . ."

That's what Susan and I talked about. What if I were convicted? What about our marriage? What about the children? They were questions that had to be discussed, regardless of how painful it was.

As the minutes plodded by, I allowed pessimism to get the upper hand, and I began assuming the worst. As we talked, I found myself cleaning out my briefcase, as if the worst had already arrived.

I said to Susan, "Here are some papers you'll need, just in case."

I handed them to her distractedly, mechanically, as if I were resigned to a prison sentence. I sorted out a few papers that I would be permitted to take with me to jail and put them in my coat pocket. The briefcase itself, with the rest of the papers, would be taken to the attorneys' office for the time being. It all seemed necessary and routine.

Then we began talking about my church membership. If convicted, my membership would automatically be revoked as is the case for anyone in our church convicted of a felony. I would lose my rights to bless my family. If it turned out to be a long sentence, who would be the father and spiritual leader in our home? To whom would the children look for a father's counsel, for a father's guidance, for a father's example, for a father's blessing?

These were hard questions to talk about, but I felt they had to be faced. Should we divorce and give Susan the opportunity to remarry, have more children, and give our other children a father in the home?

In my entire life I've never spent a more agonizing two hours. We addressed the hard questions I knew we had to face in what might be our last private moments together.

We lost track of the time, and it must have been about six or seven o'clock—maybe even later. Nearly everyone had gone out to dinner except a few like the two prosecutors who were talking and joking out in the hall.

Susan and I were still alone, and we still had much to settle. To convince her I was serious, I related to her what Sherry had told me in confidence—that Brent had told her himself that he thought that I was "going down." This was why we needed to talk about these family matters, no matter how painful.

All of this took place in spite of my father's optimism that day. He, like all of us, bore a full share of misgivings, frustrations, and worries as to the outcome during the full course of events that culminated in the trial. For some reason on this last day, he knew everything was going to be all right. He felt it and expressed it. He smiled and he laughed. He gave us confidence and comfort during those final hours of waiting. At my lowest ebb that day he reassured us by saying, again and again, "Everything's cool. Everything's going to be all right!" There was no question that he'd experienced a spiritual reassurance—something the rest of us could not yet feel for ourselves.

It was now about seven-fifteen; Susan and I, still alone, had come to the point where we couldn't say anything else; we just looked at each other and held hands. Now and then we'd hear the marshal's footsteps as he patrolled the hall.

This time the sound of his footsteps changed; I could tell he was a man on a mission, not a stroll. Since there had been some discussion about breaking for dinner and then going home, I assumed he was going to make some such announcement.

I could see his shadow on the frosted-glass door of our room. He stopped, turned, and made a general announcement to anyone who could hear.

"We have a verdict."

I was absolutely terrified!

The jury had been out only five-and-a-half hours. We had to go for at least two days, and we'd hoped for four days. Our attorneys had told us, "The sooner they come back, the worse it probably is."

I just couldn't believe it!

Susan looked at me and her face went white. She shook her head and said, "Oh, no!"

We stood up. We were both shaking as we walked over by the door. We were still alone in the room. I put my arms around Susan and said, "You'd better let me hold you because it might be the last time I'll ever get a chance."

I was holding her there for a minute when the door opened and Sherry came in. On her face was a look of complete devastation. She didn't say anything—she just stood there. She appeared to be in a state of shock.

We could hear people moving down the hall. I went across the hall to the men's room. I felt like I was burning up and wanted to rinse my face and hands.

I came back out, took Susan's hand, and we walked as slowly as we could down the long hallway to the courtroom. We held hands until I had to go through the bar, and she went to the gallery. She would have been crying, but she was too terrified to cry. Donna came over and put her arm around her.

Bill and Diane Cummings rushed back from his office after the clerk's call came on the phone. Brent got there about the same time. My parents, tired and hungry, had gone across the street for a sack of hamburgers and didn't get back in time to hear the verdict.

We sat there as the jury filed in. Brent had said to watch the jurors' eyes. If the verdict were good news, they'd look at you. If bad news, they would not.

I looked at each one of them, hoping for any eye contact. I got none until one black woman juror sat down in the front row and looked at me for a moment. Then she looked away. I thought well, they can't face me, so that's it!

At that point, I assumed that it was all over. I was "numbed out" after going through my talk with Susan that afternoon.

I looked at the jurors once again and still couldn't get a single glance in return.

Eventually Judge Williams entered and everyone was seated. The atmosphere was electric. The judge asked, "Ladies and gentlemen of the jury, have you reached a verdict on all five counts of the indictment?"

"Yes we have, your honor."

"Will the bailiff please hand the verdict to the court clerk."

This done, the clerk then handed the five-page verdict to Judge Williams. He read through all five pages of the verdict without any hint of expression on his face. We had no idea which way the verdict went.

He returned the document to the clerk and instructed the entire courtroom, "There will be absolutely no outbreaks or other disturbances in the court when the verdict is read. If you cannot control yourself, please leave the room now."

I had the sickening feeling that he was preparing us for the worst. I was being introduced piecemeal to an extended prison term by such a warning from the judge. My pulse raced, my face was flushed, I felt faint and sick all over.

"The defendant will please rise and face the jury." Brent had to help me up to my feet. I wanted to turn and catch a fleeting look at Susan before they took me down the back stairs to the prison van, but I couldn't. Would I never again hold my wife in my arms?

Would I never again, for the rest of my life on this earth, feel the sweet love of our children within the circle of our family?"

"Will the court clerk please read the verdict."

The clerk stood, cleared her throat, and began reading. "On the first count, we find the defendant, Richard Craig Smith, not guilty."

23

The Aftermath

There is no way to describe my feelings on that Friday evening, April 11th, 1986, in a federal courtroom in Alexandria, Virginia. We had won—I was free!

I was hyperventilating and didn't even hear the other four "not guilty" verdicts, but when the last one was read, I grabbed Brent Carruth and gave him a big hug. Then Bill Cumming. The courtroom went wild!

Susan wept uncontrollably, and after I kissed her across the bar, Donna took her out of the courtroom at the bailiff's request. Everyone on the defense team was a part of the victory; hugs and handshakes were everywhere. Justice had triumphed against enormous odds.

To cap the victory symbolically, Bill Cummings demanded and obtained my passport from the prosecutors.

When some quiet was restored, Judge Williams gaveled the court back to order, thanked the jury for doing a superb job, announced that my bail would be released immediately, and told me that I was free to go.

I'd never heard more incredibly delicious words in my life than "free to go."

The government attorneys, Joseph Aronica, Ken Melson, and the others, packed their briefcases and left immediately without comment, refusing to grant interviews with the media. The FBI agent who had arrested me, Mike Waguespack, shook my hand but didn't say anything.

Dr. Sherry Skidmore and Craig Smith.

The celebrating began in earnest, and it took the bailiff and marshals fifteen minutes to clear the courtroom. We almost floated down the hallway to the stairs, hugging and congratulating each other.

A moving and unusual gesture by Judge Williams took place as we were leaving. His clerk stepped into the hallway and said, "Mr. Smith, I'd like to talk to you privately, if I may." We found an open corner, and she said to Susan and me, "I have a message from the judge."

She said, "The judge felt that with all the press and the immediacy of the moment, it would be inappropriate for him to come out. But he asked me to bring this message to you. He said that he is very pleased with the verdict, and he wishes you the very best for the rest of your life."

THE AFTERMATH

* * * * *

Bill and Diane Cummings invited everyone to their home the next afternoon, Saturday, for a barbecue. My brother Hy had flown in with fish he'd caught in Florida. Peter Sylvain brought a celebration cake with the word "Hopscotch" on it, tying our victory to the famous CIA spoof-film "Hopscotch," where Walter Matthau takes on the CIA and wins.

Smith family. Left to right: Lane Smith (brother), Dorothy Smith (mother), Hyrum Smith (father), Craig Smith, Noel Smith (sister-in-law), Hy Smith (brother), Todd Smith (brother).

We all knew we would never assemble again; the feelings of affection and admiration for each other ran strong.

Susan and I spent Sunday and Monday at Bill's and Diane's cabin in the nearby hills, unwinding from the pressure of the near-disaster in our lives. It was a new beginning for us both. It was a second honeymoon.

Before leaving Alexandria, I felt compelled to thank Judge Williams personally for his courage and integrity, so Susan and I waited in that same hallway at noon on Tuesday. When his new case broke for lunch, he came out and saw us standing there.

His eyes lit up and, ignoring the press who knew me well by then, he took my hand in both of his and said, "I want you to know how pleased I am with the verdict." Then he took Susan and gave her a fatherly hug.

He said, "You've been through a real ordeal. I hope that you won't be bitter and that you'll go home and live happily and in peace."

Incidentally, his comment also served as a clincher for a decision we'd already made, not to sue the U.S. government for false arrest and imprisonment. Aside for my great respect for Judge Williams' advice and counsel, Brent Carruth put it in perspective when the government won its en banc hearing.

He said, "If the government can win CIPA appeals when the burden of proof in a criminal case is theirs, just imagine how they could jack you around for twenty years of appeals when the burden of proof in a civil case is yours. You'd be an old man if ever you saw a dime's worth of damages!"

* * * * *

A lot of great things happened while slowly traveling home to Bellevue, Washington. First we went by air to Denver for a visit with Susan's family and our children, who hadn't seen us for weeks. Then we traveled by train to Seattle. We brought the kids home from Denver by train because I wanted them to see the great United States I love so much. I wanted to get close to the land again and experience it for myself, as well.

When the train arrived, our entire church congregation met us at the station with signs, balloons and a huge limousine. We partied at the bishop's home and gave a brief report of the final day of the trial.

When we finally were driven in the limousine to our own home nearby, our friends had hung huge welcome signs all over and tied a hundred yellow ribbons on the tree in our front yard.

Home and freedom never looked better!

The Smith family home in Bellvue, Washington as decorated for the return home about April 20, 1986.

* * * * *

In retrospect I wondered why the jury wouldn't look at my eyes. I don't know. After the trial, Susan told me that when the jury filed in, one of the women, a school teacher, looked Susan in the eye, smiled, and winked. She was not yet in my range of vision, so I didn't see it. Donna Siers saw it, hugged Susan and said, "We got it."

Brent Carruth talked with three of the jurors. All three reported that when the jury first sat down after lunch with their newly elected foreman, they took a preliminary ballot and voted twelve to zero for acquittal. They spent the rest of their time going through the evidence and their notes to be sure they hadn't missed anything.

Further, all three said they were so impressed by the defense testimony that they could have voted for acquittal on the strength of that alone. Each was asked what it was that really clinched their votes. The jury foreman said, "Richardson testimony."

I received a letter from one of the jurors in response to letters of appreciation I sent to all twelve. He mentioned that one or two of the jurors were troubled with having to "convict the government" when voting for my acquittal, but their votes never wavered.

* * * * *

There are some observations to be made about press coverage. When I was arrested by the FBI on April 4th, 1984, every wire service in the nation carried my picture and the government story. The networks' evening news telecasts showed as much detailed footage of my arrest as that of any other spy bust in recent history, maybe even more. They always added the detailed particulars of the FBI's espionage charges.

The national news magazines lumped me in with John Walker and the rest of the real spies, clucking about seemingly nice people like me who were yielding to the temptation of Soviet cash.

The coverage of my arrest and arraignment was immediate and complete. I can't think of any significant news vehicle that missed it, downplayed it, or examined it with reserve or skepticism. Generally, they swallowed the FBI's story hook, line, and sinker.

The media seemed to overlook the fact that in this country a person is presumed to be innocent until proven guilty. Certainly the usual caveats—"allegedly," "accused of"—did appear in small type. It seemed everyone wanted or needed a spy bust, and the half-truths of my case looked good enough. The FBI is equated with God, mother and apple pie. Americans think it just doesn't make mistakes.

However, a few major news personalities suspected "something fishy," to quote Bob Woodward of the Washington Post. He mentioned this to his court reporter Lena Sun, who broke the true CIA story for us on page one.

Jack Anderson, ultra-blunt syndicated columnist, apparently wasn't taken in, either. Later on, Peter Jennings of ABC Television's Evening News discovered that there was another side to the CIA, but he was suddenly quiet about discussing it.

How much of what we read, see, and hear about the doings of government agencies is fed to us by the media without examination or inquiry? Has news gathering and news reporting become so immediate, so streamlined and computerized that we no longer have time to double-check our facts or suspicions?

There's an even more frightening aspect to my case. When I was acquitted on April 11th, 1986, two years after my arrest, coverage by the media was about ten percent of what it was for the arrest itself. I had no chance to clear my name in the same forum that smeared it.

My acquittal was covered locally by newspapers and the local television news in Seattle, Salt Lake City, Washington D.C., and by a few independent major papers like the Washington Post and the Los Angeles Times.

Even though mine was the first espionage case to be acquitted by a jury in the history of our country, the Associated Press chose not to report it. Were they pressured?

And even though my acquittal was a dramatic turn-around from the "over-the-fence-and-out" FBI story of two years previous, the national television network news programs only made passing mention of my aquittal. Were they pressured, too?

In spite of the fact that the mighty U.S. Justice Department embarrassed itself publicly in open court, not one national weekly news magazine published the story of my acquittal by a jury of my peers.

Time magazine carried a half-page article on my arrest, but nothing on my acquital. They finally printed a one-column-inch condensation of a letter I wrote protesting this unfairness.

Certainly my acquittal merited coverage by the same media that so eagerly covered my arrest. It was a current, newsworthy, history-making story. There was a timely opportunity to point out government excesses and overconfidence. The public welfare would be served by highlighting the near tragedy of overzealous prosecution. Why was there such inadequate coverage?

Perhaps the juror who wrote to me was correct when he reported that some jurors hated to "convict the government." Perhaps the networks, wire services, and news magazines have the same underlying reluctance to "convict the government."

A plausible assumption is that hidden pressure was brought by the government to restrain the media from reporting my acquittal in order to save government face and mend internal fences.

The ability to suppress the news is an enormous power, and centers around exchanges of privilege between the members of the media and the government. But it is not fair for the nation's news media to destroy a person's character and reputation and then, bowing to pressure, refuse to do anything to help restore these priceless possessions.

One consoling thought for me is that if I had to choose, I'd far rather have twelve conscientious jurors stand for what's right than have twelve *thousand* members of the media on my side while I was spending the rest of my life in prison!

24

My Feelings

I've tried to tell you my story as I actually lived it.

I've told you the only way we could have survived this ordeal was with God's constant help, comfort, and specific answers to our prayers.

Shortly after my acquittal I was asked to speak at an adult church meeting on Whidbey Island, near Seattle. I couldn't just get up and talk about being a spy and a hero in that kind of situation. I had to draw some conclusions, some lesson from my experience and that's what I attempted to do. This is what I told them:

First of all, nobody can give back what they took away from me. It cost me nearly $200,000 to defend myself. I spent five weeks in jail. My arrest, imprisonment, and trial caused my family three years of agony, never really knowing what was going on. I endured the sheer hell of facing contrived testimony from the FBI—people who knew me and knew I was innocent. I had to turn my back on all this, walk away, and force myself to accept it.

The simple fact is that all mankind has been faced with dilemmas since the premortal choice we had to make: whether to follow Jesus Christ or Lucifer. (Look in the New Testament of the Bible, Revelations 12:7-9).

Dilemmas are real. They are not just figments of our imagination. People in professions like police or military service are asked to take up weapons and might be compelled take a life. How does one balance that dilemma: love for and duty to country versus obligation to obey the Ten Commandments?

My own counterintelligence profession is full of moral dilemmas. How can we in that profession reconcile the things we sometimes have to do to reach national objectives with our personal beliefs and morals?

Winston Churchill, humanitarian that he was, had to sacrifice hundreds of lives one night when the Germans bombed Coventry. He knew the Nazi bombers were coming because his intelligence people had cracked the German communication codes. But to defend Coventry this one night would give away that fact, and the larger goal of winning the war took precedence. He faced a dilemma.

In my particular case what happened to me was a breakdown of the character of certain people within the system, not the system itself, so I bear no bitterness or ill will toward my country. I still love America as much as I love my own family. In fact, nowhere else in the world would the system have prevailed in righting the wrong done by these certain people.

I learned from my ordeal that we'll never find ourselves in a world without dilemmas to face and to solve. I cannot and I will not let my frightening experience dilute my tenacious pride in and loyalty to the United States of America.

It is my unshakeable personal belief that our families, our churches, and our country are inseparable, and that shrinking from the support of any of the three because we cannot cope with the dilemmas inherent therein simply adds to the problem when we should be seeking the solution.

It is also my deepest feeling that daily prayer and faith in God make possible the courage and wisdom to cope with these dilemmas and challenges.

My story is simple. I was accused by my government of one of the most heinous of all crimes, that of being a traitor to my own country. I was accused of treason against the United States of America. My government asked a jury of my peers to convict me and send me to a federal penitentiary for the rest of my life. However, I knew I was innocent, and God knew I was innocent. My faith and prayers led to miracles that resulted in the emergence of truth and the triumph of justice!

25

Did God Work A Miracle?

When I look back at the remarkable events, unusual inspirations, and unique episodes that occurred during my three-year ordeal, I have to ask myself, "Did God work a miracle for me?"

I'll freely admit that, taken individually, they were just extraordinary coincidences—each with its own unusual contribution to my eventual acquittal of espionage charges.

I'm persuaded, however, that taken as a whole and listed together, they form a pattern which show God's way of dealing with His children—especially when disaster enters their lives. This particular pattern of events is just too striking to ignore.

In looking at the events one by one, they are more than just happenstance, coincidence, or unusual events.

1. The first was my fateful phone call to the FBI's Paul Shields on June 6th, 1983. When he called the CIA's San Francisco station office at my request, he just happened to get Charles L. Richardson, whose call back to me was routinely logged. Thus it became a part of the court record that I did, in fact, talk to Richardson that day. Was it a coincidence that Richardson just happened to be in the CIA office at the time, and just happened to pick up the phone, in spite of his busy in-and-out schedule? After all, Richardson was a top-level administrator, and since he had operations going on all over

the Pacific, (including a powder-keg about to blow in Honolulu) it was highly unusual that I would talk specifically to him on that particular day.

2. Another critical event happened just a few months later when a Salt Lake City FBI agent, Pete Chase, accidentally told my former secretary, Mavis Nelson, that the FBI knew that I'd been working for the CIA. This slip provided information which was a crucial piece of evidence on my behalf, and we used it to help clinch our case at the trial.

3. Then in April of 1984, I was inspired by a Bible verse to cling steadfastly to the truth and refuse to plead the defense of diminished capacity. My attorneys had assumed that I was probably guilty or at least unable to offer proof of my own innocence. They had urged me to try for a light sentence, instead of a long jail term. But a verse from the New Testament, John 8:32, "And ye shall know the truth, and the truth shall make you free," inspired me to stay with the truth. This opened the door for a series of further truth-revealing "coincidences" to happen.

4. Bill Cummings' appointment by the court to serve as my counsel was inspired, and we felt our prayers were answered when we decided to keep him on the defense team. We struggled with this decision because it looked like I was up against a "drumhead" court, and that perhaps Bill Cummings' appointment was a part of the government's conspiracy to put me away. There is no question that someone was inspired to select an attorney who would help me, not hurt me.

5. What inspired Brent Carruth, from Van Nuys, California, to phone my mother and volunteer to fly back to Virginia at his own expense and talk to me? True, he had once taken a deposition from me in another legal matter, but this case would have been his first experience in taking on the entire U.S. government, and my prospects probably looked pretty hopeless to him. I don't know how he was inspired to pick up the phone and call my parents that day, but I

do feel that no other two attorneys in the world could have won my freedom for me.

6. Again, was it Divine providence that Judge Richard L. Williams was appointed by Judge Bryant to hear my case or was it just the luck of the draw? Some other judge could easily have let the government manipulate events to suit its own agenda. I truly believe that Judge Williams was prompted by the Holy Spirit to look carefully at both sides of this "cut-and-dried" case against me and allow me to prove the truth of my story.

7. Why did Dr. Sherry Skidmore pick up the telephone and offer to evaluate me for lie capability? After all, professionals of her rank are not ambulance chasers. Was it mere coincidence that she heard of my case and simple curiosity that prompted her call? Or was she sent to us by some "higher Authority?" Her finding, that I was programmed to be loyal and not lie, did two important things. First, my attorneys began taking my defense more seriously. Second, her testimony in court was a major factor in my acquittal.

8. Raising the $500,000 bond to get me out of jail seemed to be impossible, especially when we were so severely limited by the requirements of the court which required at least half of the amount to be in cash or bank letters of credit and the balance in deeds to real property, accompanied by current appraisals. Yet we raised the bond in just three weeks, making it possible to start my defense research before the government could sweep away the trail. A delay of another week or two could have been a disaster. I believe we were helped to make this happen.

9. Why was my CIA contact-phone number so readily traceable? We traced it to CMI on our first try. Surely our powerful government could have prevented us from tracing it successfully, or even worse, used a number which was impossible to trace in the first place.

10. We were inspired to publish the news story of my involvement with the CIA just two days before Peter Jennings broke the CIA-Bishop-Baldwin-CMI story on ABC Television's Evening News. We chose the perfect time to go public. Any earlier we would have tipped

off the prosecution and risked having our sources of evidence wiped clean. Had we waited any later, it could have looked like we were hitchhiking on the network story. Was it just a remarkable coincidence that we published my story when we did?

11. Brent Carruth flew to Honolulu and persuaded a Bishop-Baldwin clerk to make copies of all the files pertaining to that case. Days later there were raids on all kinds of CIA files, as the Agency itself began to regroup and cover up the Bishop-Baldwin affair. I'm convinced it was no coincidence that Brent beat them to these particular files.

12. As soon as Ron Rewald, key figure of Bishop-Baldwin, was out of jail on bond pending trial, Brent telephoned him. He hoped to get additional information, never dreaming Rewald would send us another whole stack of documents proving the CIA connection to Bishop-Baldwin. Why did Brent make that phone call?

13. Donna Siers just happened to be in Honolulu and overheard someone say in a chance meeting that the Rewald documents were now declassified. This information enabled Judge Williams to order the prosecution to turn over to us an entire carton containing these papers. Some of the eight documents that finally went to the jury were from this group. It had to have been more than just a coincidence that Donna overheard this remark.

14. Ken Melson, assistant prosecutor, made a slip of the tongue on the telephone with Brent Carruth on the night before the trial began which suggested witness tampering by the prosecution. This resulted in the government being forced to bring Charles L. Richardson to the courtroom. If Melson hadn't accidentally told us he'd been talking to our witness, we probably never would have gotten Richardson on the witness stand. I believe this was more than a chance mistake.

15. Joseph Aronica, the government prosecutor, became so angry he ignored Judge Williams' warning and called Richardson for cross-examination, thus allowing my attorneys to establish my CIA con-

nection and to show that Richardson had not been truthful. Was his inordinate anger just an extraordinary coincidence?

I do have the temerity to proclaim my case to be worthy of Heavenly intervention, and I know that when we look at the pattern of these unusual events, we must open our minds and hearts to the possibility that God does hear and answer the prayers of those who earnestly plead for His assistance. I know that throughout my life, there have been events in which I have been guided by God's inspiration and answers to my prayers.

The sum total of all the remarkable events and coincidences, one after another, ordered and sure, speaks of divine intervention.

It was a miracle of God's hand in mine; I cannot be persuaded otherwise.

26

How Can We Prevent This From Happening Again?

Discussions involving the investigative powers of the U.S. government usually begin and end with the assertion that the interests of a free country can best be served by that country's having the freedom to gain intelligence by any reasonable means, open or secret, which will enable its citizens to prudently act in their own national self-interest.

It is typically emphasized in such discussions that a free country cannot remain free if all sources of intelligence are simply opened up to all members of that society. In other words, we have to keep secrets from our own people.

That's why the FBI, the CIA and military intelligence are so important in keeping our nation free. No one believes this any more than I do, but there is a constant danger of excesses and abuse by those who hold such power. We can draw some important lessons from my three-year ordeal.

The highlights of my case reveal possible government abuses of this freedom to investigate secretly.

Take the breakdown of the CIA's Bishop-Baldwin-CMI Investment Co. in Honolulu. Instead of sweeping it under the rug and trying to send Ron Rewald and Craig Smith to prison to keep them quiet, why not just tell their own people the truth? Tell them that the cover has been blown and that all operations thereunder are canceled. Case officers and agents alike would understand and accept the ultimate responsibility to protect the Agency itself. They would keep this knowledge just as confidential as any other information to which they're entrusted.

A major reason for the CIA's penchant for covering up mistakes is the current movement to defang the Agency and deprive it of its powers. The CIA does have enormous powers to undertake extralegal activities to reach its objectives. But rather than force the Agency to become more and more paranoid about losing these powers, why not give it appropriate yet secret avenues through which to correct errors and adjust to changing events?

Without such internal means of modifying policy and correcting mistakes, thus righting the wrongs which inevitably creep into such a huge and complicated organization, we'll continue to see the Rewalds and the Smiths become scapegoats in the future.

This is what resulted from the cover-up fiasco in the Bishop-Baldwin case alone:

1. Charles L. Richardson went free. Any attempt to prosecute him for possible crimes committed before and during the collapse of Bishop-Baldwin, even after he admitted to having been less than truthful about his CIA dealings, would embarrass the CIA and fuel the fires of those who seek to emasculate the Agency.

2. Vital missions and operations such as mine were terminated. The stark truth is that I was well on my way to entering the KGB's spy school in Vienna, which could have led to a very deep penetration of the Soviets' intelligence community. This prize opportunity was lost forever by the furtive haste to sweep Bishop-Baldwin under the rug.

3. I was disavowed by the CIA, and thus the FBI was denied—or chose to ignore—vital information about my CIA role. Worse yet, officers of the CIA itself, may well have actually told the FBI to pick

me up for spying, to get me put away so I wouldn't ask embarrassing questions about Bishop-Baldwin and my CIA connections with their Honolulu office. This triggered their investigation of me.

4. Like Pinocchio's nose, the more the lie was told by the CIA and the FBI, the larger it grew. Soon the FBI was committed to the lie and found it necessary to investigate unfairly.

5. Polygraphs were blatantly misused over and over again to try to trap me into statements that could be regarded as confessions. Although early polygraphs by conscientious operators yielded results favorable to my case, the FBI brought in other operators who manipulated the questioning process by asking the same series of questions repetitively. Just knowing which question is coming next produces physiological reactions similar to lying.

6. The "spy bust" objective became an obsession with the FBI and biased their investigation. Agents who interviewed me were probably told what results the FBI wanted, and they were no longer committed to hearing the truth with an open mind.

7. The investigation took on a life of its own and the truth was ignored. The FBI came after Craig Smith; they didn't come after the truth. They even refused my offer to undergo truth serum and hypnosis, probably because they didn't want to hear the truth.

8. A loyal, patriotic citizen was arrested and imprisoned by his own country, and forced to spend over $100,000 to defend himself. The irony was that my arrest came because I had served that same beloved country through a highly successful CIA mission.

9. An elaborate press campaign was organized by the FBI to publicize my arrest. Those who made the decision to parade me and my case details in front of two hundred million Americans obviously knew two things. First, they knew that I really had been working for the CIA, and second, they knew that they were destroying my personal reputation and intregrity.

10. The FBI and the Justice Department used me for grandstanding in front of Congress and the media, most likely for budget-hearing purposes. Apparently they were also seeking the approval of the

general public by increasing the body count of spies caught and convicted.

11. Early on Grand Jury and pre-trial procedings were completely one sided. Evidence that I was working for the CIA was either ignored or suppressed. By this time the Cia mess in Honolulu was starting to leak out, and the Agency was desperate to have me put away for a while. The government, needing another spy bust to satisfy Congress and the public, was only too happy to oblige.

12. The amount of my release bond was set unreasonably high, possibly in violation of my constitutional rights. The first federal judge, perhaps responding to the government's heavy-handed use of my story of contact with the Soviets, first established a cash bond of a half-million dollars. This would have effectively prevented me from getting out of jail and researching the facts supporting my own defense. Obviously, this was the purpose of the government's request for an unreasonably high bond figure.

13. The first of two instances of witness tampering or evidence suppression occurred when Robert Madsen, psychologist and federal employee, was threatened by the government with the loss of his job if he testified concerning his psychological evaluation of my probable loyalty. His data, which suported that of our own private forensic psychologist, Dr. Sherry Skidmore, was quashed by this threat.

14. The second instance took place when a major network news anchor apparently "encouraged" by government pressure on ABC to discontinue his investigation and exposure of Bishop-Baldwin's ties to the CIA after only three program segments were aired. It was obvious to anyone watching and listening to the televised interviews with various people involved with Bishop-Baldwin: employees, investors, Ron Rewald himself, and his prison guards, that the CIA was getting the worst possible exposure of their runaway Honolulu operation. Obviously, certain people in the government felt that something had to be done to stop this hemorrhage of embarrassing information, and suppressing the investigation was a good place to start.

15. An innocent citizen was almost sent to prison for life. Perhaps this was the most outrageous excess of all because it's obvious that both the CIA and the FBI knew that I was innocent— innocent but expendable. The "greater good," that of hiding the misdeeds of government officials, was served at the expense of an innocent pawn.

16. Government officials apparently ordered break-ins of my apartment and my attorney's office to obtain evidence to be used against us. We knew we could never prove government involvement so we had to ignore it.

17. To suppress evidence that was embarrassing to the government, the prosecutors invoked the Confidential Information Procedures Act, CIPA, in my trial. This was unfair and unwarranted since, in this case, there were no security issues in any of the documents we discovered and presented to the court. CIPA should never be invoked just to cover up government error and embarrassment.

18. Similarly, when Judge Williams acted correctly and denied their motion to invoke CIPA, the prosecutors appealed to the Fourth Circuit. Again, this was wholly unfair and unwarranted because of the lack of security issues in these documents.

19. Finally, when this appeal to the Fourth Circuit was denied, they asked for and got an en banc hearing before all twelve judges of the Fourth Circuit. We can only speculate as to what kind of political pressure was brought to bear because after sixteen months of silence they voted seven to five to overturn the two previous decisions to deny CIPA protection to the government. Thus the FBI finally won the right to invoke CIPA and quash our four hundred pages of evidence linking the CIA with Bishop-Baldwin, even though these documents were ruled "relevant," "admissible," and "essential to a fair trial" by both the trial court and the three-judge tribunal of the Fourth Circuit.

20. Taxpayers' money was wasted extravagantly for all of these lengthy proceedings plus the runaway costs of the government's prosecution at my trial. The prosecutors spared no expense in staging a flamboyant parade of extraneous people and superfluous graphics

at the trial, to the consternation of conservative and economy-minded Judge Richard Williams.

21. It appeared that the government prosecutors had prepared scripts for their FBI witnesses which attempted to twist my CIA story into confessions of various sorts. Our defence attorneys repeatedly had to ask the judge to force the witnesses to refrain from reading prepared scripts during the trial.

22. The news of my acquittal was deliberately and methodically suppressed by the government. The action taken against it by a courageous jury received only ten percent of the publicity that was given to my arrest. Thus the government not only destroyed my character and reputation, they prevented the news media from taking any significant steps to help restore it.

All of the expensive, illegal, and—most important—life and freedom threatening events could have been prevented if only I'd been told of the existence of the problem with Bishop-Baldwin in Honolulu.

Three very important questions are raised: Should "saving government face" be placed above an innocent citizen's safety and free pursuit of happiness? Should a citizen who has placed his life on the line for his country be forced to choose between his duty and his freedom? And should not we all be able to have an unshakable faith in the honesty, fairness and integrity of our government?

It's mind-boggling to imagine that knowledgeable government officials would stand by and watch me drown, just to avoid embarrassing certain people, their offices, and their agencies. Such callous indifference to the rights of a loyal citizen against unfair prosecution for acts performed in the line of duty should, in itself, be punished. Why not threaten to give a forty-year prison term to those who would stand by and let a citizen be so prosecuted?

Guarding against the unfair deprivation of life and liberty are the very tenets that motivate our most courageous and patriotic risk-takers to aid their country.

I know that I can't propose specific changes in the laws to bring about this kind of equity, to insure that a case of injustice like mine is never allowed to happen again. That's the job of those who make the laws and write the regulations that oversee our intelligence agencies.

Our lawmakers and our executive branch can, and they should, look at my case and find a better balance between the security of national defense and the personal freedom of those who are caught out in the cold through no fault of their own. Our leaders must take action before someone is hurt permanently.

If my experience were to be the catalyst for such change, then it would be worth all the risk, all the expense, and all the tragedy of my ordeal. I hope and wish with all my heart that this will be the outcome of my trial by fire.

Index

A

ABC Evening News—143, 146, 207, 214, 220.
Agency, the (see CIA)
Ala Moana Park—80, 86.
Alaska, State of—27.
Alexandria, VA—7, 107, 109, 123, 124, 127, 138, 139, 142, 152, 156, 161, 162, 177, 201, 204.
Alexandria Field Office, FBI—106 (Photo), 107.
"All the President's Men"—142.
Ambler, Eric—28, 29.
American Express—186.
Anderson, Jack—207.
Arizona, State of—19, 21.
Aronica, Joseph, Prosecuting Attorney—130, 159, 166, 167, 168, 169, 179, 180, 181, 182, 183, 184, 186, 188, 189, 191, 192, 193, 201, 215.
Associated Press—207.
Austria—75.

B

Bailey, F. Lee,—156.
Ballard, M. Russell, 162.
Bellevue, WA—96, 97, 105, 108, 111, 138, 139, 151, 153, 204, 205.
Berlin, East—134.
Berlin, West—134.
Bible, Scriptures—113, 115, 117, 209, 213.
Bishop, Baldwin, Rewald, Dillingham and Wong (Bishop-Baldwin)—82, 86, 89, 141, 143, 144, 146, 147, 158, 159, 160, 172, 173, 175, 180, 181, 183, 184, 189, 190, 214, 215, 217, 218, 219, 220, 222.
Bolivia—44, 45.
Brigham Young University, BYU—19, 162.
Bryant, Judge William—128, 129, 130, 132, 144, 145, 214, 220.

C

California, State of—44, 46, 116, 163.
Camelback Mountain—174.
Carruth, Brent, Atty—15, 116, 118, 119, 120, 124, 125, 126 (Photo), 130, 132, 133, 134, 135, 137, 140, 141, 142, 144, 145, 146, 147, 150, 153, 154, 157 (Photo), 158, 162, 165, 166, 167, 168, 171, 172, 175, 176, 177, 178, 179, 181, 182, 183, 184, 185, 186, 187, 189, 190, 191.
Cavannaugh, Richard P. (see Charles L. Richardson)
Central Intelligence Agency (see CIA)
Chase, Pete—111, 165, 169, 172, 173, 190, 213.
Christ, Jesus—115, 209.
Christian—23, 29.
Churchill, Winston—210.
CIA, the Agency, Central Intelligence Agency—7, 19, 23, 28, 33, 35, 36, 41, 42, 45, 46, 52, 53, 57, 59, 63, 65, 66, 73, 74, 79, 81, 82, 83, 84, 85, 86, 87, 88, 89, 90, 91, 92, 93, 95, 96, 97, 98, 102, 103, 108, 111, 112, 115, 116, 119, 123, 126, 127, 128, 134, 135, 139, 140, 141, 142, 143, 144, 146, 147, 151, 152, 153, 154, 158, 159, 161, 165, 166, 172, 173, 174, 180, 181, 185, 186, 189, 190, 207, 212, 213, 214, 215, 217, 218, 219, 220, 221, 222.
Classified Information Procedures Act (CIPA)—148, 151, 155, 158, 159, 160, 164, 177, 204, 221.
CMI Investment Co.—80, 86, 140, 141, 143, 144, 146, 147, 159, 172, 173, 181, 184, 190, 214, 217.
Communist—17.
Cooney, Lloyd—122.
Coventry—210.
Cummings, Bill—114, 116, 118, 123, 124, 125, 126 (Photo), 128, 129, 133, 134, 138, 139, 141, 142, 145, 150, 153, 154, 156, 157 (Photo), 158, 162, 168, 169, 171, 172, 178, 184, 186, 187, 192, 198, 201, 203, 213.
Cummings, Diane—156, 198, 203.

D

Danny II—80, 86, 134, 140.
Danville, CA—83.
Davis, Mike and Sherry—30, 32, 43, 44.
DeGrasse, Tony—45.

DeLorean, John—162.
Denver, Co—20, 123, 162, 204.
Dulles Airport—102, 106, 165.

E

Europe, Eastern Europe—75, 77, 78, 128.
Evidentiary Discovery (Rule 16)—145, 146, 147, 164.
Excelsior Hotel—93.
Explorer Scouts—32.

F

Fairfax County, VA, Courthouse—107 (Photo), 108, 109 (Photo).
Fairfax County, VA, Jail—7, 20, 110, 113, 115, 118, 126, 173.
Far East—47, 53, 76, 78, 80, 161.
FBI, Bureau, Federal Bureau of Investigation—14, 16, 20, 23, 27, 28, 66, 77, 82, 84, 85, 86, 87, 88, 89, 91, 93, 94, 95, 96, 97, 98, 99, 100, 102, 104, 105, 106, 107, 108, 109, 111, 112, 117, 119, 121, 128, 139, 141, 153, 154, 158, 161, 164, 165, 166, 167, 169, 172, 174, 185, 188, 190, 192, 201, 206, 207, 209, 212, 213, 217, 218, 219, 220, 221, 222.
FBI Headquarters Building—99 (Photo).
Federal Building, San Francisco—26, 83, 91.
Federal Building, Seattle—94 (Photo).
Federal Communications Commission, FCC—143.
Florida, State of—46.
Fourth Circuit Court of Appeals—150, 151, 155, 159, 160, 172, 175, 177, 178, 221.
Friederichstrasse—75.

G

Germans—210.
God, Heavenly Father, Lord, Heaven—29, 32, 43, 44, 97, 112, 114, 115, 117, 118, 130, 153, 154, 155, 162, 207, 209, 210, 211, 212, 216.

H

Harvard Law School—125.
Hawaii, State of—27, 64.
"Her Husband's Mistress"—30, 66.
High Uinta Mountains—32, 43.
Hilly, Ron—93, 95, 165.

Hoffman, Mark—84, 165.
Holy Ghost—117, 214.
Hong Kong—46, 70, 77, 80, 134, 135.
Honolulu, HI—59, 60, 63, 64, 76, 80, 81, 82, 86, 89, 90, 112, 134, 140, 143, 144, 146, 159, 173, 174, 181, 184, 189, 190, 213, 215, 217, 219, 220, 222.
"Hopscotch" (Movie)—203.
Humphrey-Trong—123.

I

"I Led Three Lives"—18.
Ilikai Hotel—64 (Photo), 65.
Iowa, State of—157.
Ishida, Danny—33, 37, 38, 39, 42, 46, 47, 50, 52, 56, 59, 63, 80, 82, 85, 160.

J

Jacksonville, FL—16.
Japan, Japanese—7, 19, 20, 21, 22, 25, 27, 33, 34, 36, 42, 43, 45, 46, 47, 49, 50, 52, 53, 54, 57, 59, 62, 71, 77, 78, 80, 85, 89.
Jarvik, Robert—46.
Jennings, Peter—143, 144, 146, 207, 214, 220.
Jerusalem—162.
JETRO—45.
John, the Apostle—117, 155, 213.
Jones, Noel—26, 36, 92, 165.
Justice Department of (See United States of America)

K

Keio Plaza Hotel—57, 58, 71, 72.
KGB—7, 18, 33, 37, 40, 47, 48, 53, 59, 74, 75, 76, 85, 86, 89, 119, 134, 135, 143, 175, 186, 218.
KIRO Radio and Television (CBS)—122.
Kokhlov, Nicolai—134, 135.
Kremlin—82.
KSL—CBS—171.

L

Langley, VA—98.
La Scala Coffee Shop—50, 51 (Photo).

Laurel, MD—25.
Library of Congress—140.
"Light of Day"—28, 29.
Lincoln Memorial—18.
Logan, UT—16, 19.
Los Angeles, CA—39, 43, 56, 125, 132, 135, 144, 173.
Los Angeles Times—207.
Lowe (Bishop)—118.
Loyola University Law School—125.
Lucifer—209.

M

Madsen, Robert—133, 135, 220.
Marshall, Ted—34, 35.
Maryland, State of—26, 92, 101.
Matthau, Walter—203.
McLean, VA—118, 185.
Melson, Ken—168, 169, 176, 201, 215.
Miko Coffee Shop—70, 71 (Photo), 72.
Minor, Paul—165.
Monson, Augusta—17, 43.
Monson, David (Lt. Governor)—48, 49, 59, 70.
Monterey, CA—19.
Monterey Language School—19, 20, 62, 101.
Mormon Church, LDS, Mormon—28, 83, 124, 137, 162, 185.
Mormon Temple—19.
Moscow—41, 72, 73, 134.
Murphy, John—95, 98, 165.

N

National Park Service—141.
National Partners of America—44.
Nelson, Mavis—111, 112, 119, 165, 172, 173, 175, 179, 190, 213.
New Otani Hotel—33, 47, 70.
New Testament—117, 209, 213.
New York, State of—121, 123.
Nixon—142.
North Salt Lake City, UT—44, 88.

O

Okunev, Viktor—53, 55, 56, 57, 58, 64, 65, 68, 70, 71, 72, 73, 74, 75, 76, 77, 78, 79, 82, 85, 95, 134, 161.
Orem, UT—93.
Osaka—45.

P

Pacific Grove, CA—19, 101.
Pacific, Pacific Rim—85, 152, 173, 181, 213.
Pacific Plaza Hotel—94.
Paris—19, 76.
Peace Corps—23.
Philbrick, Herbert—17.
Phoenix, AZ—20, 174, 176.
polygraph(s), poly(s)—91, 92, 93, 94, 95, 98, 99, 102, 103, 165, 219.
Presidential Gardens—138, 139.
Provo, UT—19, 20, 23.

R

Revelations, Book of—209.
Rewald, Ronald—86, 146, 147, 158, 159, 160, 173, 177, 179, 180, 181, 184, 215, 217, 218, 220.
Rexburg, ID—20.
Richardson, Charles L./ Cavannaugh, Richard P.—80, 85, 86, 87, 89, 90, 140, 147, 159, 164, 165, 172, 173, 174, 175, 176, 177, 178, 179, 180, 181, 182, 183, 184, 185, 190, 193, 206, 212, 215, 216, 218, 221.
Richmond, VA—150, 151.
Rome—76.

S

St. Francis Hotel—59, 68, 69 (Photo).
St. Louis, MO—143.
Salt Lake City, UT—16, 17, 25, 31, 43, 59, 68, 70, 78, 80, 84, 85, 89, 91, 111, 123, 124, 137, 162, 165, 168, 171, 172, 190, 207, 213.
San Francisco, CA—26, 27, 29, 30, 36, 38, 39, 40, 59, 60, 68, 69, 70, 78, 83, 85, 86, 88, 91.
San Roman, CA—26.

Shmitz, Bill—94, 98.
Schwendiman, Fred—162, 170, 184.
Scotland—16.
Scriptures (see Bible)
Seattle—91, 93, 94, 100, 105, 204, 207, 209.
Seventh Adventist—162.
Severn, MD—25.
Sherrill, Charles—171.
Shields, Paul—83, 84, 85, 86, 87, 88, 89, 119, 165, 193, 212.
Shinjuku—49, 57.
Siberia—41, 134.
Siers, Donna—156, 157 (Photo), 158, 159, 162, 163, 171, 179, 185, 187, 198, 201, 205, 215.
Silvain, Peter—141, 157 (Photo), 162.
Skidmore, Sherry (Dr.)—132, 133, 134, 135, 141, 157 (Photo), 162, 170, 172, 179, 187, 192, 197, 198, 202 (Photo), 214, 220.
Smith, Craig and Susan (Susan Woods)—7, 9, (Photo), 13, 14, 15, 18, 19, 20, 21, 22, 23, 25, 26, 29, 30, 31, 33, 34, 35, 38, 40, 51, 52, 62, 63, 64, 65, 66, 67 (Photo), 68, 78, 79, 80, 81, 82, 83, 84, 85, 86, 87, 88, 89, 90, 91, 92, 93, 94, 95, 96, 97, 98, 99, 100, 101, 102, 103, 110, 111, 112, 113, 115, 120, 124, 125, 126 (Photo), 127, 128, 130, 132, 133, 134, 136, 137, 140, 143, 145, 153, 154, 155, 159, 161, 162, 165, 170, 171, 172, 173, 184, 185, 187, 188, 189, 190, 191, 193, 196, 197, 198, 199, 200, 201, 202 (Photo), 204, 205 (Photo), 206, 207, 208, 209, 210, 211, 212, 213, 214, 215, 216, 217, 218, 219, 220, 221, 222, 223.
Smith, Aubrey, Brittanie, Ian, Sunny, children—14, 20, 30, 31, 32, 113, 153, 155, 204.
Smith, Hyrum Mack II and Dorothy (Monson), parents, Dad, Mom—16, 17, 18, 31, 97, 100, 101, 111, 112, 120, 121, 122, 124, 125, 130, 136, 137, 139, 140, 141, 145, 152, 162, 187, 197, 198, 203 (Photo), 213.
Smith, Hyrum Mack III (Hy, Hydie), Lane, Todd, brothers—17, 18, 64, 118, 122, 123, 125, 128, 136, 138, 139, 140, 143, 162, 170, 187, 203 (Photo).
Smith, Terry, sister—19, 136, 162.
Smith, Becky, Noel, sisters-in-law—64, 203 (Photo).
Smith, Rick—88, 89, 90, 91, 92, 93, 165, 166, 167.
Smith, Joseph, Prophet—16.
Smith, Joseph (Doctor)—20, 101, 102, 157 (Photo), 162.
Soviet(s), Russian(s)—7, 14, 16, 33, 40, 41, 42, 48, 49, 50, 54, 55, 57, 59, 60, 63, 69, 70, 73, 75, 77, 79, 82, 85, 92, 93, 94, 96, 97, 98, 108, 115, 119, 128, 134, 143, 161, 174, 186, 189, 206, 218, 220.

Soviet Commercial Compound—41, 50, 51, 53, 54 (Photo), 58, 70, 72.
Soviet Consulate, San Francisco—39, 40, 59, 70, 164.
Soviet Embassy, Tokyo—40, 47, 48, 49, 50, 53, 54, 55, 58, 71, 77, 89.
Soviet Intelligence—75, 143.
Soviet News Agency (see Tass).
South Africa—164.
South, Southern—123.
Styler, Harriett—168, 169.
Sun, Lena—142, 143.
Switzerland, Swiss—77, 78.

T

Taipei, Taiwan—46, 48, 59, 70, 72, 77.
Takanaba Tobu Hotel—51, 52 (Photo), 53.
Tass, Soviet News Agency—48, 49, 50.
Temple Square—166.
Ten Commandments—210.
Terminal Island, CA—173.
Timespan—44, 46, 47, 68, 77, 78, 85, 88, 172, 186.
Time Magazine—208.
Tokyo, Japan—20, 21, 22, 33, 34, 38, 39, 40, 45, 47, 48, 49, 51, 52, 54, 60, 64, 69, 70, 71, 75, 77, 84, 85, 164.

U

U.C.L.A. Psychology Department—132, 134, 135.
United States of America, U.S.A., U.S., American(s)—7, 13, 27, 34, 35, 37, 39, 40, 45, 46, 49, 56, 68, 75, 77, 79, 80, 82, 83, 97, 108, 109, 114, 123, 128, 138, 153, 161, 162, 165, 174, 184, 185, 186, 189, 204, 207, 210, 211, 219.
United States Air Force—28.
United States Army Intelligence—7, 16, 19, 20, 21, 26, 30, 32, 34, 36, 56, 75, 165, 217.
United States Army Intelligence Special Operations—26.
United States Army Intelligence Headquarters—20, 25, 27, 28, 32.
United States Army—19, 20, 22, 27, 28, 83, 186.
United States Congress—104, 148, 219, 220.
United States Defense, Dept. of—25.
United States District Court—124, 127, 128, 138, 159, 161, 177.
United States Education, Dept. of—18.
United States Embassy—33, 45, 134.

232   ACCUSED

United States Government—14, 33, 36, 41, 62, 92, 112, 125, 143, 146, 150, 151,
    153, 154, 155, 166, 175, 181, 189, 190, 191, 204, 208, 211, 213, 214, 217, 220,
    221, 222.
United States Justice, Dept. of—108, 110, 114, 121, 129, 132, 145, 161, 207, 219.
United States Navy—16, 28.
United States Supreme Court—151.
Ushijima, Mr.—34.
Utah, State of—32, 34, 45, 46, 47, 78.
Utah-Bolovia Partners—44.
Utah, Hotel—166, 169.

V

Van Nuys, CA—124, 213.
Vienna—74, 76, 76, 77, 79, 81, 85, 86, 218.
Vietnam, War—19.
Virginia, State of—18, 83, 98, 111, 121, 123, 124, 125, 133, 146, 213.
Voice of America—134.

W

Waguespack, Mike—94, 95, 96, 97, 98, 101, 102, 103, 104, 106, 165, 166, 202.
Waikiki—64, 65, 66.
Walker, John—174, 206.
Washington, DC—18, 20, 25, 66, 91, 98, 105, 123, 207.
Washington Post—142, 143, 207.
Whidbey Island—209.
White House—18.
White, Ken—33, 34, 35, 36, 37, 38, 39, 40, 42, 45, 46, 47, 48 49, 50, 56, 59,
    60, 63, 64, 65, 70, 73, 76, 79, 80, 81, 82, 83, 84, 85, 86, 87, 134, 135, 140,
    172, 173, 190.
Whitworth—174.
Williams, Judge Richard L.—8, 15, 129, 130, 135, 138, 144, 145, 146, 148, 149,
    150, 151, 152, 154, 155, 158, 160, 161, 162, 163, 167, 168, 172, 275, 276, 177,
    178, 179, 180, 181, 182, 183, 186, 199, 201, 202, 204, 214, 215, 221, 222.
World War II—16.
Woods, Mitchell—115, 162, 204.
Woodward, Bob—142, 207.

Y

Young, Brigham—16.